Charles Klosterman

TO BUILD A CHURCH

TO
BUILD
A CHURCH,

by

John E. Morse

Introduction by
E. A. Sövik, F A I A

Holt, Rinehart and Winston
NEW YORK · CHICAGO SAN FRANCISCO

Library of Congress Catalog Card Number: 68-10073

FIRST EDITION

Designer: Bert Waggott
SBN:03-065475-0
Printed in the United States of America

—◦◦{ ✻ }◦◦—

Acknowledgments

No book of this kind is possible without the help of a number of persons—and this one is no exception. I am indebted to E. A. Sövik, FAIA, not only for writing the Introduction, but for his helpful criticisms of the manuscript. Portions or all of the manuscript were also read by Professor James F. White, the Rev. Scott T. Ritenour, Robert E. Rambusch, Mildred Widber, John R. Potts, and the Rev. James L. Doom. Their comments and criticisms have been invaluable. Dr. Howard E. Spragg, Executive Vice President of the United Church Board for Homeland Ministries, his immediate predecessor, Dr. Truman B. Douglass, and Dr. Purd E. Deitz, General Secretary of the Board's Division of Church Extension, were most supportive of the enterprise at many crucial points. The encouragement of William Robert Miller and the late Rev. Lawrence M. Upton were major factors in my undertaking the preparation of the manuscript. While the support of all my colleagues was essential to its completion, special acknowledgment is due to August Burchardt, who was jointly responsible for the preparation of Appendices I and II.

Portions of this book have appeared in the *United Church Herald,* publications of the United Church Board for Homeland Ministries, and material prepared by the Board of Christian Education of the United Presbyterian Church in the United States of America, and used here with permission.

Preparing a manuscript while discharging one's usual responsibilities is chaotic at best—and only the patience of my staff, particularly Aimee Paterno, Ruth Esther King, Lillian Churgin, and Audrey Parker made it possible. I am also grateful for the loyal help of my mother, Mrs. Milford J. Morse, who typed the final manuscript. Joseph Cunneen and Catherine Oleson, of the staff of Holt, Rinehart and Winston, not only carried out their responsibilities with care, but their sensitive guidance was most helpful at many points in developing particular themes and concepts. For the help of these and many others I am profoundly grateful.

JOHN E. MORSE

March 17, 1969

TO

Mary Jo—

AND OUR

John, Mary, and Jennifer

--⋅◄ ❋ ►⋅--

Contents

INTRODUCTION   xiii

PREFACE   xvii

PART I: BUILDING WITH UNDERSTANDING

Chapter One: To Build a Church   3

Why churches build—Consequences of failure in church building—Basic questions for every building program—Effect of changing patterns of society—New understandings of Christian mission—Polarities and ultimate impossibility of building a church—Churches as places for worship, education, service—Importance of environment sensitivity—Qualities essential to good church architecture

Chapter Two: Churches in the Midst of Change   16

Societal changes require new concepts of church building—Character and effect of contemporary changes—New understanding of a church's parish—Changes in laity—Possibilities for decentralized programs and buildings—Advantages of shared facilities—Planning and erecting buildings ecumenically—Importance of need-centered buildings

*Chapter Three: Buildings That Reflected Belief—
and Some That Did Not*   24

History as a measure of church architecture—Ancient pagan worship compared to early Jewish practices—Temple and synagogues and effect on early Christian worship—The "house church"—Emergence of Christianity in Rome—Veneration of saints, the *martyria*—Early church leaders and art—Catacomb drawings as first Christian art—Effect of Constantine's recognition of Christianity—The basilica—The Middle Ages—The Gothic church—"Canterbury" style and separation of people and clergy—Character of Gothic churches—Renaissance and Reformation—Churches of

Christopher Wren—Puritan meetinghouses and their effect—Imitative patterns of nineteenth century—Auditorium-type buildings—The Akron plan—Revivalist individualism and Gothic romanticism—Birth of contemporary religious architecture—The "modern" movement—Essential questions for good church architecture in any period

Chapter Four: Of Art and Symbols   38

Art as a valid expression of religious men—Estrangement of art and the church—Artistic fundamentalism within the church—Unsatisfactory character of "religious" pictorial art—Pictorial and abstract art compared—Appropriate decorative functions of art—Stained- and colored-glass—Art used for purposes antithetical to the church—Process for selecting or commissioning art—Architecture as an art form—Guidelines for appreciating contemporary art forms—Symbols compared and defined—Symbols that become clichés—Transient and disposable art—Architecture as a symbol—The "church that looks like a church"—Today's innovation as tomorrow's convention—Self-defeating efforts to create architectural symbols

PART II: ARCHITECT, BUILDING COMMITTEE, SITE,

AND MASTER PLAN: CRITICAL CONCERNS

FOR THE BUILDING ENTERPRISE

Chapter Five: A Key Person: The Architect   51

Qualities of a good architect—Importance to the building enterprise—Reasons for employing an architect—The church "package deal"—Working with architect as a learning experience—Advisability of selecting architect at an early stage—Respective roles of architect and building committee—Compensating the architect for his services—Using architect's time wisely, fairly, and creatively

Chapter Six: The Written Program   60

Written building program essential to good architecture—"Program" defined—Building program for remodeling projects—Various methods for developing building program described and compared—Guidelines for program study committees—Varieties of study committees needed—Their election or appointment—Source materials needed—Importance of written conclusions—Content of written building program—Involvement of architect in its preparation

Chapter Seven: Selecting the Site 66

Objective criteria for church sites—Importance of subjective criteria—New church sites—Ultimate questions in evaluating appropriateness of sites—Church sites and co-operative church planning—Comity differentiated and described—Failure of comity—The "one-mile" rule and results—Regional planning contrasted—Importance of research—Site requirements resulting from new understanding of mission—Considerations of size and shape—Importance and effect of zoning and deed restrictions—Geographical barriers—Traffic patterns—Location of school and streets—Visibility—Topography and soil conditions—Involvement of architect in site selection—Utilization of sites that do not meet all objective criteria

Chapter Eight: The Master Plan 75

Importance of site master planning—Dangers of overplanning—Master plans need not be detailed—Continuity and coherence of style—Testing and evaluating proposed master plan—Parking requirements and the master plan—Location of parsonage on site—Landscape planning—Desirability of church basement—Correcting mistakes of the past—Architect's extra compensation for master plan—The "first unit"—Pros and cons of various possibilities weighed

PART III: FORM, FUNCTION, AND BELIEF

Chapter Nine: Places for Worship 85

Traditionalism as the temptation of worship committees—Fundamental questions for worship committees—Public and "privatized" worship differentiated and defined—The liturgical movement and its effect on architecture—The church as a gathered community—The secular use of church buildings—Effect of appropriate spatial qualities on worship—Multiple foci for worship—Inappropriate accouterments
    The altar/table, its historic use and importance—Altar rails—Protestant confusion concerning communion—Relationship to other foci of worship—Importance of place for preaching of Word—History of preaching and evolvement of pulpit—Preaching distinguished and defined—Relationship to other foci of worship—Baptism—Varying concepts and interpretations—Principles of location and design—Baptism by immersion and architectural implications
    Location of Bible—Development of lecterns and reading desks—Congregational hymn singing as act of worship—Problem of where to locate choir

—Role of choir in worship—Architectural solutions for "choir problem"—The organ—Location—Electronic versus pipe organ—The "human factor" in building design—Considering the physically infirm or incapacitated—Seating problem and requirements—Limitations resulting from the use of pews—Places for private worship—Chapels and their use

Chapter Ten: Space, Form, and Christian Education   108

Task of Christian education—Implications of broad definition of Christian education—Human needs as concern of a Christian education building committee—Relationship between Christian education and the church at worship—Designing spaces for functions while preserving flexibility and options for future modification—Square footage recommendations commonly accepted—Spatial qualities required for Christian education—Multiple use of facilities—Art and Christian education—Unhappy experiences with church-school art—Potentiality of children's "art"—Effect of ecumenical movement—Pioneering ventures in shared education facilties and other experiments in teaching forms and practices—Audio visuals—Using facilities other than church buildings for education

Chapter Eleven: Places for Community Service   124

Problem of "fellowship" buildings—Limited concepts of fellowship— Meeting halls rather than fellowship halls—Need for inventory of existing community facilities—Needs should be defined in terms of persons as well as organized groups—Practical considerations in designing meeting halls— Stages and kitchens—Libraries and their use—Parlors and their place— Youth activities and needs—Places for administration—Their importance and uses—The minister's office and his study

Concluding comments: The servant church as the Church incarnate for our day

NOTES TO TEXT   130

APPENDICES   134

   I   How to Conduct a Building Needs Study   134
  II   Critical Questions in Selecting a Church Site   146
 III   How to Select an Architect   150
 IV   Financing the Building Program   153

BIBLIOGRAPHY   164

PARTIAL LIST OF DENOMINATIONAL ADDRESSES   170

–•≪ ✳ ≫•–

Introduction

Covarrubias, the artist of a generation ago, once brought to Shanghai a fine and ancient Mexican piece of jade carving. It occurred to him that it was much like the work done by good Chinese jade carvers, and in a conversation with a Chinese connoisseur who was also impressed with the similarity, he agreed to show it to a group of art dealers. Covarrubias' Chinese friend took the carving to a meeting of these men, where it became the subject of a prolonged discussion. The art dealers had not been told that it was Mexican, and when Covarrubias arrived at the meeting he found them sitting around a table on which the jade piece was resting, in a great argument about which dynasty had produced the carving. None of them suspected that it was not Chinese.

To Covarrubias this was evidence that, contrary to general attitudes, taste is not a subjective and personal thing. In two widely separated cultures, each plying primitive tools to work the same material, thoughtful and skillful artists produced work that is impressively similar. Good taste may be an intuitive matter, but it is the intuition of wise and perceptive people, and such intuitions are not whims or fancies.

This is part of the reason Eric Gill has said that bad taste is the worst heresy. Bad taste is the judgment of the naïve, or unskillful, or insensitive, or thoughtless. It fails to see relationships, and results in disorder, lack of integrity or wholeness.

The other reason Eric Gill could make this statement is that he saw art as a means of communication. Heresy is not only a matter of written creeds. Visual arts can also communicate. A good work can express truth. A work which is in bad taste is an assertion of untruth. Good work can reveal the whole and the holy; bad art is a denial of integrity and order. Such a denial is heresy because it is inconsistent with faith in a God of holiness and order.

In a conversation following a conference during which the author of this book and I had been talking with a group of ministers about church building, he made the comment that even if the ministers took their work seriously, and even if one spent a great amount of time exploring the problems of architecture with them, this would not assure them of good churches. What is essential are good architects. In the end it is the architect who puts the space and substance together. And if his taste is not superior the building can be a sort of heresy.

It is just as true, however, that a good church does not necessarily result whenever a good architect enters the work. It is quite possible for a building to be a good work of art but a poor tool for the parish. For instance, I have recently seen two examples of churches designed by eminent and able architects which are archaic in their liturgical arrangements. And insofar as a church building fails to be a good tool its value as a work of art is also diminished, for the best architecture is a union of tool and symbol, and the perfection of each enhances the other. That which serves well speaks; that which speaks truth, serves.

The clearest success doubtless comes when the best dialogue between earnest client and able artist has prepared for it, when each illuminates and regards the other, when the client informs the architect most fully and explicitly of his purposes, and the architect gives the form to the structure.

The work of art comes from the hand of an artist, not from a committee, and it is rare and difficult. Not infrequently, committees are insistent if unwitting impediments to its achievement. This circumstance is such a hazard and so frustrating to the designer that often there is truth in the drafting-room graffito: "My client is the enemy."

A church building, as a tool, has a complex and difficult purpose. It is useful not only in the sense that it efficiently shelters the activity of the congregation, but also in the sense that it informs and forms the spirit of the community, reinforces their common mind, reflects their ideals, echoes their hopes, amplifies their sense of common destiny, encourages their faith, supports their enterprise, and defines their commitment. A building cannot do this unless its designer is both sympathetic to, and sophisticated about, the life of the community. He must learn to know them well so that he can give form, not to his own but to their purposes.

It is the virtue of this volume that it can prepare both client and architect for the dialogue and common effort. It is the best book on this subject yet published, and the parts which deal with the relationship of committee and architect are particularly well done.

People who know Morse will expect to find both knowledge and wisdom. It will surprise them, as it did me, to learn that a good deal of the writing took place during the months when he was also performing skillfully the endless duties of chairman in preparation for the first international and interfaith congress on religion, architecture and art. Although he is neither architect nor cleric, but a lawyer, the author's churchmanship as well as his visual sensitivity are apparent; and it is particularly satisfying that in a time of uncertainty and frustration in the church a voice so lucid and hopeful should be heard in an area which is sometimes thought of as a wilderness.

E. A. Sövik

Northfield, Minnesota
January, 1969

---※---

Preface

"Churches' Spires, Arches Must Go." "Congress Scores Architecture." "No More 'Country Club' Churches." "Want Moratorium on New Cathedrals." "Church Building Styles Outmoded." "People, Not Churches, Sacred." "Architect Criticizes Church 'Unreality.' "

These are but a few of the headlines generated by the first International Congress on Religion, Architecture and the Visual Arts held in New York City in August 1967.

Fifteen or even ten years ago such headlines would have been unimaginable. We were then engaged in the most frantic, extensive church building boom since the London fire of the 17th century. But today, despite the large sums still being spent on church buildings, many religious leaders are having second thoughts. Even such a person as Fulton Sheen, a Catholic bishop and long a success figure in the religious establishment, is waging a vigorous campaign against the construction of multimillion dollar churches and the "edifice complex" which he asserts these represent.

More than one architect and professional religionist has reacted defensively and with dismay at this change in emphasis. For example,

Philip Johnson, one of America's leading architects, made an eloquent plea to the International Congress for a new era of building great religious edifices, but he was immediately challenged by a clergyman who arose from the audience and told Mr. Johnson that this statement clearly proved he was not the right architect to design his church—a position with which many delegates agreed.

The protesting clergyman probably represents the thought of most contemporary theologians; the evidence is strong that those who seek to build new cathedrals will find it increasingly difficult to obtain the necessary popular or ecclesiastical support. Large in scale, costly to construct, difficult to maintain, poorly suited for new worship patterns, cathedral-like church buildings are rapidly becoming anachronisms. While the reason given for halting work on the Cathedral of St. John the Divine in New York was the need for funds to combat the urban crisis, it is at least debatable whether the vast sums required to complete the Cathedral can ever be justified on a rational basis.

Contrary to the scare headlines, the sober judgment of the delegates attending the Congress was not to stop building churches, but to stop putting up structures that are inadequate for the work which the Christian church should be about. That is essentially the position of this book. It does not assume the irrelevance of church buildings; on the contrary, buildings can be most important in helping churches carry out their mission responsibilities.

Some "practical" churchmen may wonder how a book on church building can be helpful without a myriad of pictures, drawings, and the like. If a committee wishes to study pictures, there are a number of volumes described in the list of sources in the Appendix which will fulfill those desires. The basic premise of this book, however, is that design should grow out of program, not out of a book of pictures or group of blueprints. Thus the task of the building committee is to describe the real needs of the church, which are the consequence of its beliefs and the action those beliefs require. The responsibility of the architect, on the other hand, is to interpret the church's program through an appropriate design. An excellent design solution can be expected by those churches that carefully develop and define their programs and entrust the design solution to a capable architect who is sensitive to their requirements. If this book can in some measure help architects and churches to achieve that result, then it is a practical book in the best sense of the word.

—◦◦❧ ❋ ❧◦◦—

PART ONE

Building With
Understanding

Good church building committees and architects
are by nature iconoclastic and are open-minded
to every new possibility. Fresh thinking and
new ideas are indispensable. One cannot create
a good building simply by repeating
time-honored formulas.

--◦◦◦ ❊ ◦◦◦--

CHAPTER ONE

To Build a Church

"It is arguable that to build churches for cultic occasions only can be a
self-regarding 'spiritual' luxury, when millions of men and women
are suffering from lack of material assistance." [1]
—*J. G. Davies*

Few undertakings offer as many possibilities for creativity, or greater
risk of failure, as building a church.

Churches erect new buildings for a variety of reasons. The newly
gathered church seeks to provide a place that will meet its basic need
for shelter. If it already possesses a building, it may be inadequate to
carry out the tasks that are the responsibility of a church. The building may have been designed without understanding or inspiration; resulting inadequacies may actually impede the church in its work as a
community that worships, learns, and shares. A building may no longer
be adequate or function satisfactorily for a congregation which takes
seriously new concepts of mission that emphasize the servant role of the
Christian community. Something more may be needed than a traditional
sanctuary which can serve only as a place of Sunday worship.

There are other reasons why some churches must rebuild. Existing
buildings may have been planned on the basis of inaccurate projections of future growth; there may be need for more space, or, as is more
often the case, the building may have been planned on the basis of
overly optimistic expectations and must be replaced to avoid wasteful

expenditures for maintenance and repairs. Some churches may find it necessary to relocate and rebuild, but many relocations appear to be cases of churches seeking to avoid involvement in community and social problems which they must otherwise confront.

Despite those who would summarily dismiss church buildings as unneeded and undesirable, most persons who seek a meaningful relationship to God and their fellow man require a place in which these relationships can be nurtured through worship, learning, sharing, and participation in a common mission. To provide a place that truly meets these requirements is well worth the cost. Although some church buildings stifle the human spirit, churches can also be places of expectation, confrontation, and renewal, where people gather as a visible community in order that they may be prepared for the tasks to which God has called them.

Failures in church buildings are not difficult to observe. They may be seen in buildings where the real purpose of pastor, or parishioners —or both—was to achieve recognition by their community and denomination; in structures whose design and construction were apparently dictated by laymen who saw the building process as strictly a business matter with no relationship to faith, mission, or even traditional churchmanship. On more than one occasion architects have succumbed to a tantalizing opportunity for architectural sentiment and romance, reflecting the concerns of another age, with no conception of the direction of contemporary theology; others have created pseudo-medieval fortresses to last an eternity, despite the ease with which church buildings become obsolescent at an early age.

Failures such as these are usually unsatisfactory from an aesthetic standpoint, but the institutional stagnation they reveal is even more serious. Poor church buildings are essentially the result of poor churchmanship. Most of these failures could have been avoided if pastor, parishioners, and architect had a better understanding of what it means to build a church today.

Basic Questions for Church Building

To build a church for these times it is not enough for the architect and building committee to possess a superficial acquaintance with the history of religious concepts. Our understanding of these concepts is itself in the process of change as a result of today's radical re-examination of many of the basic assumptions on which churches have historically operated. The church can no longer be thought of as a holy domain divorced from the world about it, presided over by an all-knowing clergy and a small number of laity who represent an ingroup. Nor is it any longer possible to understand the church solely in denominational terms, for what we vaguely call the ecumenical movement may prove to be the most important development in Christianity since the Reformation.

And, in addition to institutional and theological change, the church finds itself in the midst of a society which is itself undergoing massive change. The urban revolution, the demise of small, rural communities, the rising expectations of the black and other minority people, the apparent immobilization of many suburban churches, all are examples of changes that will inevitably affect all of our institutional forms, including the church.

The first inquiry in every building project must therefore be related to basic questions. What is the task of the church today, i.e., the mission God has given to it? What forms is the church called to take? In what ways is the church made manifest in contemporary society? What is the claim of God today on churchmen who would be obedient to his will?

Effect of Contemporary Changes

Until recently, most Christians seemed to believe that the church somehow possessed an exclusive channel through which God carried out his purpose. Today we have a greater sense that God works in many ways and places, through many forms of organizations and institutions. Ministry should no longer be fixed to a particular location but should be of a fluid nature, moving rapidly from place to place as the mission of God calls it. The church is suddenly faced with the fact that it has no security in a claimed authority to be the exclusive instrument of God's will but, rather, stands under the same judgment that faces all men and all institutions. The day is gone when it can meet the tests of judgment by pointing to the "conversion power" of the minister.

Nowhere is the challenge to the church more clearly demonstrated than in the field of church building. In an age of fluid requirements, a building might seem to freeze the work of the church to a particular piece of ground, thus preventing the institution from carrying out its larger responsibilities. As we have seen, some have even concluded that church buildings are no longer appropriate, and that to build at all when the church is in a state of transition is to waste resources by creating an irrelevant and unnecessary structure. And it is all too apparent that in some situations buildings are a hindrance to effective ministries.

Bishop Sheen is not the first or only person to suggest that a moratorium be placed on church building so the sums saved can be used to help solve our social problems. Today fewer seminary graduates are seeking positions in the parish ministry; many cite as a reason their fear that they will be caught in an institutional round robin of erecting a building, followed by a concentrated effort to pay off the debt so the church can build again, thereby acquiring more debt. One critic has correctly pointed out that the size and nature of the church plant, more than any other single factor, will determine not only how the pastor will spend his time but the kind of program the church will offer the community.[2]

Not Too much

Churches that seriously consider these questions may react in several ways. Accepting the principle that a church need not have a building to be a church, one group may become convinced that, because they do not have a building, they necessarily have a deeper sense of mission—a twist which undermines the commitment that initially brought the group together. Other churches may decide they must build, but guilt arising from this decision so haunts them that the building becomes a fruitless exercise in abnegation. Economy is equated with stewardship. Christian service is measured by how much money has been saved, and the quality of mission is demonstrated by the degree to which aesthetic concerns are ignored. Such pocketbook righteousness is often accompanied by a rejection of art as a necessary or desirable component of church building. Even when some provision for art is put in the budget, priorities are such as to force the church to satisfy its requirements with catalog art, or by commissioning works of mediocre artists.

Not all churches react in this way. Some go to the other extreme, and since nothing is considered too good for God, lavishness and opulence become the pattern. They confuse their building needs with those of the designers of the Houston Astrodome. If baseball merits a little gold and glitter, surely some of the same will earn a few merit badges with the Lord!

In a fundamental sense, it is really impossible to build a church. Architects are asked to provide a permanent structure in the midst of transiency, and avoid obsolescence in an age in which obsolescence is a basic assumption. Builders are supposed to erect structures that are houses for people and also houses where God confronts his people. Buildings must be erected for the future, when no one can foresee the future. Designers are challenged to represent the transcendent spatially in a world where orbiting satellites have rendered virtually meaningless attempts to symbolize God's presence by creating vaulted roofs, massive towers, and lovely spires. Church buildings are expected to be places set aside for the worship of God at a time when men increasingly see God in terms of human needs and in other contexts which are more secular than sacred. Men are told they should not build monuments in a culture which is constantly reminded of its debt to the past through monumental forms and institutions.

People who build churches should begin by recognizing the ultimate impossibility of the task, but obviously they cannot stop there. Although confronted by contradictions and temptations, it is also their task to find out what guidelines exist. They must ask fundamental questions in the hope of receiving answers that may lead them to find the best solution that can be achieved.

Buildings Are for Worship

To build a church is to create a place for worship.

Most building committees, left to their own resources, invariably place worship as the number one activity that justifies the existence of the institutional church, and some would argue that the provision of shelter for worship is in itself sufficient justification for erecting a new church building.

Perhaps that is so, but the essential question remains: What is meant by worship? J. Gordon Davies has suggested that to build churches for cultic occasions can only be a self-regarding "spiritual" luxury. And there is substantial evidence that many people are no longer willing to underwrite the cost of this kind of "luxury." Hundreds of empty pews, even at the "prime" time of 11 o'clock on Sunday morning, give convincing evidence that the churches have not always kept pace if their goal is significant worship experiences.

Many critics of the "traditional way of doing things" suspect that one overriding reason for this apathy is the tendency of much of our Protestant worship to degenerate into cultic practices devoid of substantial meaning. The Roman Catholic Church has recognized this situation and has attempted to meet the problem by instituting new forms of liturgy which actively involve the laity in its celebration. Although the same kind of problem exists among Protestant churches, there is only limited evidence that it is a matter of great concern. In spite of declining church attendance in many areas, worship has continued to follow traditional patterns that are empty of contemporary meaning. For some, worship has become simply a thoughtless repetition of outdated practices; for others, an exercise that provides a platform for a minister who still believes he can change the world through polished and learned expositions. The results can be either monumental boredom or a congregation that is held together by the spellbinding magic of a strong personality. When such churches erect new buildings, the design most often reflects their doubts and confusion about the purpose and validity of worship.

That these doubts and confusion have found their way into American church buildings is evident from the criticism that has been leveled at them, particularly at that portion of the building which is sometimes described as the reason for its existence—the place of worship. The late Dean Samuel Miller, of Harvard Divinity School, believed that much of our contemporary religious architecture was "architectural vaudeville, comic renditions of what should be religious sanctuaries." [3] Another typical comment is that of the noted architect and critic, G. E. Kidder Smith, who described the new churches erected in this country as generally the "most fumbling and desperate ever erected," and argued that "far too many are warmed-over 'Gothic' or 'Colonial' or ill-conceived, ill-lit, ill-constructed pastiches, seemingly designed to startle, be photographed of a May morning and forgotten a year later." [4]

Probably the basic issue troubling most persons is whether or not worship should be restricted to traditional cultic practices, or broadened to permit a wide variety of activities that will more truly relate the issues of life to man's worship of God. Those who argue for the latter believe that unless this is done the church could well become a museum piece, irrelevant to the issues of our lives. In order to truly relate worship to man's life style, the concept of worship must be enlarged to include an emphasis on the totality of life—our mutual responsibility for the social and economic problems of today, the rights of the disenfranchised and the outcasts, as well as our need for expression through a variety of forms such as dance, music, film, drama. Active congregational participation is a necessary prerequisite. The key is flexibility, to permit a wide variety of expressions rather than a week-to-week somewhat monotonous order of worship that is seldom changed to any significant degree.

The dilemma is that we of the laity, who control much of the direction a church can take, intuitively resist change and innovation, particularly in the area of worship. We tend to shy away from anything that disrupts or changes patterns to which we have become accustomed. Neither do we appreciate worship experiences which fail to soothe and which may even jar our sensibilities. It is another story, however, in our business and social lives; there we are quick to adapt to new situations lest we be left behind. Other considerations come into play in the church; we become dogmatic and rigid, and close out all opportunities for experimentation and innovation. Worship is surrounded by a special aura which seems to defy all efforts at variety or modification.

Contemporary religious architecture relates to this problem in an unusual way. It is often said that some of the most daring buildings house some of the most conservative congregations—a statement that probably contains more truth than most would care to admit. Examined closely, most contemporary churches do not reflect true innovation and experimentation in the design of the interior of the place of worship. Adequate provision is made for traditional practices—but rarely is there any provision for the new forms of worship which many younger clergymen and laymen long to see as part of their worship experiences.

Imaginative architectural forms are not enough to create a satisfying place of worship, especially if they act simply as shields for irrelevant traditionalism. Unless there is a genuine newness in the worship life of the Christians who meet there, which in turn is reflected in the church's design, the building will probably convey a pervading sense of falseness. Our basic plea is for a wholeness in contemporary architecture—contemporary in form to meet the requirements of contemporary practice.

To worship in the old meetinghouses of New England can be a far more refreshing and helpful experience than to worship in many so-called "modern" churches. At least the form is honest and consistent with the needs and practices of the people who built the structures. There is no element of pretense or falseness; the buildings are what they are: simple, tasteful places for people to meet who wish to gather in worship or work. This example suggests there is an eternal relevance to a building that reflects an understanding of religious values of the time in which it was built, even though erected many years ago; but a building designed with little comprehension of the world in which it is placed or the needs of the people who will worship there will forever be haunted by the falseness with which it was originally conceived.

Many causes could be given for the tendency of much contemporary architecture to fail in essential matters, but they are rooted in one fact—many church buildings are planned by architects and building committees who do not see the importance of thinking along fresh lines on what it means to worship in today's society. As a result, the "ill-conceived, ill-lit, ill-constructed pastiches" are at odds with the basic need of people for a place in which they can come to a meaningful relationship with God. Buildings that appear to be contemporary structures, but in fact reflect beliefs and practices of previous generations, are outdated the moment they are dedicated. There is no way they can avoid the ultimate criticism that a failure to build with sensitivity to contemporary needs produces results that are a barrier instead of an aid to faith. It might be better to relegate worship to purely secular surroundings.

Buildings Are for Teaching

To build a church is to provide a place where people can be equipped, through teaching, for their tasks as participants in the community of faith.

Just as concepts of worship are undergoing re-examination and are being broadened beyond traditional rituals, so is our understanding of Christian education assuming new meaning. Once seen as a classroom for youngsters, Christian education is increasingly seen in a new perspective. It is no longer simply teaching; it is an integral part of the church's ministry, its task that of equipping people for their role as Christians in everyday living.

Here again history is disturbing. There is substantial evidence that each generation tends to build educational facilities for the needs of the previous one, with the result that American Protestant churches never seem to catch up with the times. Churches have gone through the "central assembly" period, in which young people were gathered for opening exercises followed by dispersal to small classrooms; the "cubbyhole" period of tiny individual rooms for the teaching of biblical history; and the "specialized classroom" period, in which rooms were provided for every conceivable age group from the very young to adults. Many churches are still in this latter period, although there is evidence of a changing approach that would move Christian education out of a "Sunday school" context and into a more realistic environment. Our commitment to the past has left us with hundreds of obsolete church-school buildings that require rebuilding or extensive remodeling with each generation. It is clear that every church which builds needs to devote much of its time to an examination of its present program, then make an imaginative attack on the problems of the future.

Buildings Are for Service

To build a church is also to build a place for service.

The most profound implications of what it means to be the "servant church" are lost if it is understood only to mean making bandages for hospitals, preparing gifts of food for the poor at Thanksgiving, and gathering toys for unfortunate children at Christmas. This type of activity is commendable, but it can be little more than a palliative to the conscience of churches that ride easily on a secure financial basis. Ultimately, service calls for a churchmanship that conceives of its responsibilities as going far beyond the good intentions of the ladies' guild or social-action committee.

One of the clearest manifestations of the Christian church is the bond of brotherhood that binds its members together. Unfortunately, most of the trappings of traditional church brotherhood impede a true understanding of what is meant. The reality encompasses something more than Rotarian camaraderie or Masonic loyalty. Anyone who has worked in a parish knows only too well that churches tend to equate this kind of fellowship with service, and defeat both fellowship and service with pleasant chitchat, monthly suppers, and rummage sales. The church should be a place where fellowship does not depend on such activities but grows out of a life of significant service by persons who hold a common faith.

When the Mercer Island, Washington, United Church of Christ planned its new building, the committee spent many hours discussing the implications of Christian service for the building program. It soon became evident that committee discussions could lead nowhere until the advice of community leaders was obtained. Representatives of the State Child Welfare and Family Services were invited to meet with the committee. Members of the city's planning commission, officials of the YMCA, and other civic leaders were also asked to give counsel. It soon became apparent that some of the assumptions on which the committee had operated were false, and needs which the church could meet were discovered that otherwise would have been overlooked. This careful homework is paying dividends as the church builds a structure which will be used many hours during the week for a variety of programs.

Every situation has its special needs, whether it be a child-care center, a day nursery, a place of recreation for teenagers, places for the elderly to read, work, or pass the time of day. And there is more than one community in which the church could serve an extremely useful purpose by providing places for programs designed to cope with broad community problems, many of which can be funded through government programs.

The scarcity of church buildings that evidence any planned concern for the responsibilities of the servant church is mute testimony of our failure to understand Christian discipleship in its fullest dimension. In recent years, however, there has been a growing suspicion that perhaps the only true life in Christ is that which is found in the lives of others. At times, this renewed concern for humanity has been motivated by the guilty knowledge that the "institutional" church has lived most of its life as a receiving institution rather than one that gives of itself. In some cases, old buildings have been remodeled and new programs instituted to care for the needs of the entire community, not just those who belong to the church. In increasing numbers, congregations are becoming restless in the knowledge that their buildings, which lie unused six days a week, constitute a potentially valuable resource for the whole community—they could be utilized to accomplish many things that need to be done but for which people have previously been forced to depend exclusively on government and local charities.

Qualities Essential to Good Architecture

Along with its concern for the needs of the world, the congregation preparing to build should be sensitive to the environment in which the church will be placed. Martin Marty has spoken of the "fortress church, claim-staking, imperial, self-seeking, pretentious, misplaced, overextravagant, competitive, attention-getting." Building such a church leaves behind a "concrete example" that "will not be shouted down by preachers' words and parishioners' actions." [5] There is no excuse for lush, fat church buildings that are nothing more than exercises in ego satisfaction. There is no place for "imperial" buildings that proclaim self-righteousness and smugness; they effectively contradict everything the church can say about the Gospel.

It is just as important for a church building committee to set forth the qualities that are needed in a church building as it is to list the classrooms that will be needed in the church school. Some buildings welcome people; others do not. Some buildings invite all to enter, regardless of race or social or economic position; they seem to proclaim that a people of faith are gathering here. They reveal a concern for the problems of the community. They are sacred places that are still very much a part of the world.

Other buildings are clearly retreats from the world, but some are quite subtle in their exclusiveness. One common example is the church that is designed to serve only one segment of society to the exclusion of all others. The favored group is frequently the family consisting of married couples with young children. Facilities are provided solely for this group on a lavish basis to meet every conceivable need, with insensitivity to the needs of those who are childless, unmarried, or perhaps not formally affiliated with the church. The saccharine advertisement proclaiming that a family that prays together will always stay together has become for many a symbol of the church, although it suggests that the ministry of the church is to serve its member families to the exclusion of other needs which are often as serious and basic to the church's mission.

Congregations with an overwhelming conviction of their own self-importance may be tempted to seek publicity from editors who respond to the unusual or exotic in architecture. A building that attracts the curious but does not serve its role as a place in which committed people are gathered is not a church but a museum, worth study, perhaps, as an example of building skills but not for its Christian role. Equally destructive are those efforts to enshrine Christian belief in self-consciousness, prettiness, or cuteness.

Building churches also offers temptations to architects and churchmen who perhaps unconsciously wish to create a monument to their own wisdom and foresight. The result may be a building that drains so many resources from the church that no money is left to finance programs or employ adequate staff. Such a building soon becomes a mausoleum for beautiful dreams destroyed through inept planning. To erect a church that makes impossible the needed program is to ensure early obsolescence.

Although church buildings should not be planned as an eternal monument, they should, of course, remain usable for a reasonable time; otherwise the cost of depreciation becomes ridiculous. History, however, confirms that church buildings usually require major remodeling and even rebuilding after thirty or forty years, and any attempt to build for permanency beyond such a period is probably fruitless. With few exceptions, the day of building cathedrals to last for generations is over. Our technological and cybernetic age causes yesterday's miracle of construction to become quickly obsolete.

Obviously, there is no "authorized" list of Christian qualities that must be found within a church building. Each congregation should carefully study the meaning of the Gospel for today and develop a list of those qualities that seem most important. The architect who receives such a list should not dismiss this as an exercise in theological jibberish but accept his responsibility to create buildings that not only serve the church functionally, but symbolically proclaim the essence of the Christian Gospel as his client-church has perceived it.

There was a time when the building of a new structure was automatically one of the hallmarks of a successful ministry. The complexity of the task, the administrative skills required, the popular support and response to a building program, served as badges of merit to validate a ministry.

But the story is different today. More than one parish minister has found himself frustrated and defeated by an undertaking which usually results in a financial demand of major proportions for years to come. Seen in its negative aspects, building a church is an exercise in futility, presenting impossible claims on the minister's talents and energies. As a result, some have opted for buildingless churches, that is, churches which meet either in temporary structures or those designed principally for non-church programs. The results of these efforts are mixed, but in some situations they have proved successful, not always in terms of numbers, but in the effectiveness of a relatively small group of people.

In the last analysis, however, the question is not whether men should build churches, but what kind of churches they should build. Men cannot build out of a complete understanding of their mission and the extent of their servitude, because this is beyond their full comprehension. They cannot build to reflect the God they worship; this, too, is outside the realm of possibility. Churches are built because people who gather must be housed, but there is more to it than that. Men build because God has given us talents, spirits, and aspirations which we feel compelled to express in creative forms. We build because we cannot *not* build.

The God we worship has given us a mission, a portion of which is to understand him and ourselves in our relations both horizontally and vertically, and to share that understanding in service with and for mankind. Therefore, it *is* appropriate to express in our art forms as much as we understand of our God, ourselves, and the world about us. Man's dilemma, God's redemption, our response in obedient mission—these are the expressions of the church in the 20th century. Our task is to build as best we can, knowing that complete success is not really possible. Our task is to do the best we can, knowing that God judges our failure to achieve less severely than our failure to go forth in obedience with whatever insight we can develop.

—◦◦∜ ✳ ∦◦—

CHAPTER TWO

Churches in the Midst
of Change

"If there is to be a religious art and architecture, it will not be found in
any attempt to plant these meanings and values into blobs of paint and
pieces of steel by cunning craftsmanship and ingenious symbol-mongering.
There was a time when this strategy worked. The artist or architect today
who looks to the religious community to supply him the right nuts is
likely to find his mouth full of mush." [1]

—*Daniel Callahan*

*What symbols
speak today*

M ost churches seem to approach building programs with an eye
to the past and apprehension about the future. Even those
church leaders with some awareness of the revolutionary developments in contemporary Christianity seem to be saying: "My church, it
never changes!" Although there is no automatic benefit to be derived
from change unless it reflects a new plan of attack in discharging
responsibilities for mission, any church that boasts "We're still doing
it that way" has seen change only as a threat, not as an opportunity.

Notwithstanding the evidence which justifies Mr. Callahan's skepticism of the ability of churches to cope with these issues, churches cannot safely ignore the implications of change, especially when building
programs are involved. Buildings are necessarily designed for the future,
not to serve the past. Change cannot be ignored; the future of many

churches may rest on the care with which building committees perform their tasks of studying its nature and effect.

Social change has also been accompanied by an outpouring of theological thought which is remarkable in its content and implications. The subject has aroused substantial popular interest, and many magazines have carried rather exhaustive articles on the implications of change for religious institutions. Comment has varied from those few who have espoused a "death of God" theology to a careful examination by an authority such as Dr. Joseph Sittler, of the University of Chicago Divinity School. Paul Tillich even suggested that today was a time of "God's freedom from religion, even his fight with religion." [2] Bonhoeffer, to whose thought much of this ferment can be traced, argued that we are "proceeding toward a time of no religion at all," [3] and Sittler has described the "erosion and displacement of value" [4] which seems typical of our style of life.

Running through much of this writing is a central theme which has captivated the imagination of many. The ancient power and heritage of the church are not forgotten or discounted, but to many it is not enough to appreciate the historical role of the church. Some fear the death of the church, although giving no credence to the "death of God" statements. Most would argue strongly that for the church to be the church, it must be broken open to the needs and concerns of the world, and not permitted to remain symbolically or illusionistically protected within the walls of cherished buildings.

These are obviously not remote matters of theological speculation but the most important concerns of a church that is considering a building program. It goes without saying that the claims of the critics should not be accepted automatically, but to build without consideration of their position is to run the risk of putting up new churches that are an anachronism on the day they are dedicated.

Those who demand a broadening of the church's ministry are calling into question several traditional assumptions. One such assumption is that primarily the church should serve a parish that can be defined in terms of streets, distances, and natural barriers. This kind of geographic parish, usually residential, has been Protestantism's main base of operations for most of its history. As Americans become more and more mobile, however, we have become involved in activities and concerns that cut deeply across all segments of society. In an increasingly urbanized world, the church has found itself touching only a narrow portion of a man's life and interests—those related to his place of residence.

One of the reasons for the demand that the church expand beyond self-imposed residential parish boundaries is the claim that only as people relate to others is Christ truly Christ, and that the most significant human relationships are often found outside the usual residential parish. Thus the church that constructs a building in the expectation that God will somehow come to its door is indulging in fantasy. Tillich has stated that such churches build for "the absent God . . . who has withdrawn in order to show us that our religious forms in all dimensions were largely lacking both in honesty and in consecration."[5] In its simplest terms, this concern for the secular is a demand that the church relate itself compassionately and with comprehension to the full spectrum of human needs. Seen in this light, it is nothing more—and nothing less—than an injunction that the church open itself to changing shapes of need and new forms of hope.

Before this can be done, however, churches must understand the character of the majority of the laity today. The church is sometimes described as a gathered community, but it is a dispersed community as well. It gathers for some of its functions, but its members go to many other places for work, learning, and the other activities of life. At one time, most people lived, worked, and died in the same community. The church was often the center of life, and the church building came to symbolize this centrality: the church on the green in New England, at the crossroads in the Midwest, and on the principal avenues and streets of our cities. The church was the place for the town meeting, the natural center for many cultural, educational, and recreational activities.

But today, urbanization and its attendant mobility have created a new kind of world and a new kind of laity. Suburban husbands spend most of their time in places other than where they live, and it is no longer unusual for a family to travel a great distance on any weekend in search of recreation. The result of these new patterns is frequently detachment and noninvolvement with the issues of the residential community—and disinterest in the church that confines its ministry to that narrow base.

This is also an age of education and affluence, in which more and more churches have narrowed their horizons to those of the middle class. People less educated or less fortunate economically are often relegated to groups not related to the major denominations, notwithstanding the fact that many of these persons have related historically to Protestantism. Overtones of racial exclusiveness are often present, as minority groups are discouraged by acts that overtly or by subtle implication discourage participation in the typical church in a "good neighborhood."

The gap between middle-class America and the socially and economically disadvantaged has widened to a point where the values of the former are sometimes confused with Christianity. Although this highly mobile and broadly educated middle class sets many of the standards for our churches, it has far less loyalty and commitment than was the case several generations ago. Many who are church members seem to think of the church somewhat as they do the Red Cross—a worthwhile organization that merits some economic support but hardly a center of action and personal commitment. What commitment exists is often limited to an organization, a building, or a minister.

At the same time, the church has on a variety of occasions demonstrated its moral power by acting strongly and without equivocation in the cause of social justice. At times this power has been directed toward legislation; in other cases, local community organizations have sought and received vital support. The problem is not one of lack of persuasiveness. Rather it is one of marshaling the power which is resident within our institutional structures.

This opportunity for greater effectiveness has convinced many that the church must take some radical steps to break out of its present strait jacket. There is broad agreement that the church restructure itself to respond to needs in ways that cannot be done by a frozen and immobile organization.

It should be clear that the kind and location of church buildings will be highly important, either as support or impediment, in developing this broader understanding of the ministry. There are no easy prescriptions, but several principles should be kept in mind.

If ministries are to be broadened, churches must be prepared to decentralize both their program and their buildings.

Decentralization is not a new concept to American society. Factories and department stores do not hesitate to build where they can most profitably carry out their activities. Neither has American education found it difficult to decentralize its campuses in order to meet expanding challenges. With few exceptions, however, the local church has not solved the problem of how to break out of one location and take its program and buildings where they are most needed and will be the most effective.

Decentralization would mean more specialized types of buildings, and probably smaller ones. They would not necessarily be less expensive, especially if the church returned to the central city, where land and construction costs are generally higher. Considerable savings could be realized, however, by reducing the scope and size of many "church plants" that dominate our residential neighborhoods. If space uses are properly planned, it should not be necessary for a church to have as large a building in one location as now seems to be the case. Decentralization of program need not always require new buildings. In some cases, community-owned buildings may be available; in others, it may be possible to rent adequate facilities. Some may fear that decentralization would mean de-emphasizing the worship function of the church, but it is difficult to see how a church could carry out its mission responsibly without adequate provision for worship in all segments of its ministries. The significant question is whether we can all broaden our ideas of what constitutes a "churchly" place for worship.

Broadened ministries may require the church to build facilities that can be shared with others, including profit-making organizations.

One of the reasons often given for the unwillingness of a church to venture into areas that are already built up (such as the downtown portions of major cities) is the high cost of land and high construction costs. These need not be determining factors, however, if a church is willing to join with others who have some of the same problems to solve.

Some churches are experimenting with buildings that are shared with others. The American Lutheran Church organized a new church on Waikiki Beach, Hawaii, one of the most expensive pieces of real estate in the United States, and solved the problem of land costs by combining the church with a high-rise apartment building for retired people. The United Church at Niles, California, is relocating to a site that is part of a shopping-center complex. Also, hotels and office buildings have been combined with accommodations for church functions with varying degrees of success. Other churches have solved the parking dilemma by working co-operatively with business groups.

The number of churches that have experimented along these lines is limited; most are reluctant to venture into these co-operative relationships, even when land costs are staggering. Perhaps this hesitancy is due in part to the church's assumption that it is an institution that builds outward and never upward. Prudent stewardship of valuable land dictates that the church be willing to build vertically, with the church and the other organizations dividing the cost in proportion to the value of the space occupied. Failure to see that a church can build "up" can lead a congregation to conclude that it cannot afford to go forward with its plans for ministry but must retreat to some safe, secure sanctuary.

No one will deny that building horizontally is usually easier, but the crucial decision comes when a church must decide whether to build vertically or not build at all—and thus abandon an entire field of ministry. Teaming up with others can sometimes solve problems of land acquisition and cut construction costs. Of course, legal issues are to be considered, and the taxation situation must be carefully studied; this kind of decision requires careful but imaginative thought. Despite the difficulties, however, there are more possibilities inherent in "vertical" churches than many churches seem to realize.

Broadened ministries will require the church to plan programs and erect buildings ecumenically, whenever possible.

Ecumenical co-operation among denominational mission boards has been increasing at a rapid rate in recent years, with the result that many major projects undertaken nationally are now sponsored by two or more denominations. While the growing spirit of ecumenicity has without question been helpful, saving money has probably been the most compelling motivation. The denominations have found they cannot afford to duplicate programs and that better projects at less cost are possible when they work together.

Local churches should be able to work together with just as much effectiveness. Co-operative programing will relieve many of the budget problems created by broadened ministries, and better programs should result from broadened financial support. Possibilities for improved facilities at less cost through ecumenical co-operation are obvious: less building will be needed, and the buildings that are provided can be more efficiently used. In a study of the possibilities in ecumenical co-operation in one new town, Columbia, Maryland, Dr. Stanley Hallett, formerly Executive Secretary of the Department of Church Planning of the Church Federation of Greater Chicago, has pointed out that the money saved by erecting buildings that could be jointly used by the denominations in their Christian education program is sufficient to provide a five-day-a-week church school with a professional paid staff at no additional cost. A large number of denominations have joined with the Archdiocese of Baltimore to implement Hallett's proposals. And in Kansas City, the properties of First Congregational and First Presbyterian churches were sold and the proceeds used to erect a new facility to house an inner-city program supported by the Episcopal and Roman Catholic dioceses, as well as the United Church of Christ and the United Presbyterian Church.

Broadened ministries will require that churches erect need-centered buildings.

The need to worship and the need for Christian education should be obvious to every church, but other needs are not so obvious. Each person on a committee involved in a building program should be encouraged to use his imagination and suggest possible programs for every need that could conceivably be met by the church. Many suggestions will not be workable, and priorities will eventually have to be established. But the basic question to be asked, not once but repeatedly, is: What are the needs in the lives of people that this church should and could meet?

Churches can be shortsighted in describing those who should be served, and at the outset often limit themselves to their present membership. While a church should know something about its own membership, it is far more revealing to study those who are not members but whom the church should be serving. Most churches have a vast untapped reservoir of people who need the church—and whom the church needs—but both church and people may proceed through life without recognizing each other.

People have traditionally sought out the church at the "high points" in their lives—at baptism, confirmation, marriage, and burial. Churches can grow careless in discharging even these basic responsibilities, as when its church buildings do not provide a proper environment for these ritual occasions.

Other areas of concern are easily overlooked. For example, many churches have developed needed ministries in nursery school and day-care centers, but fewer have shown any interest in providing services and ministries to those groups of children not usually found in these centers: the brain damaged, the physically handicapped, the retarded. Many programs serving disadvantaged persons can be financed with funds from public and other nonchurch sources, but the church might provide required buildings and personnel resources. There is a whole range of opportunities that represent a challenge to the lay talent within the churches and their still largely unused buildings.

The need to provide significant programs for teenagers demands careful study. Here again, the church must enlarge its concerns beyond the small group of young people who still come to Sunday school, and be willing to minister to youth without demanding either membership or loyalty in return. Many churches have found their most successful ministry is simply to provide a place where teenagers can gather in relatively unstructured situations. Some adults may be disquieted by a seeming lack of "religious content" in these programs, but churches which have experimented in this direction report that few programs of Christian education have brought greater satisfaction.

Another area of need is that of young adults, particularly the unmarried young adult. Few churches have bridged the gap that separates twenty-year-olds from the church until the loneliness of being unmarried brings them back; or, in the case of young married couples, until the most confining responsibilities of child rearing are behind them. Usually, ten years of a person's life go by in which the church plays no part in helping him understand and accept himself. Yet this is a time when the church could perform a great ministry if it could find ways to build a bridge.

Another group of which the church should be aware is composed of adults thirty-five years and older—persons who for varying reasons have remained unmarried. The church can be cruel in the way it develops its programs around the family or the married couple, with the unmarried person expected somehow to tag along. Those of retirement age also find it difficult to fit into the typical family-oriented church. It is not enough to provide "circles" in which the older women can meet, or "hobby rooms" where older men can while away their hours, although places for meeting and rooms for various activities can be of real assistance. Churches should ask themselves whether they are simply providing for busyness or are thoughtfully trying to meet the requirements of those without adequate opportunity for self-expression and continued development.

There are other kinds of needs that can be easily overlooked. It is not an absence of religious feeling that keeps those who are economically, socially, or racially disadvantaged from beating a path to the church. Only those churches that are aggressively seeking to serve their community, however, may find them.

—◦◦{ ❀ }◦◦—

CHAPTER THREE

Buildings That Reflected Belief—And Some That Did Not

"'The [church] building must be theologically sound, esthetically
satisfying, and psychologically suitable to the people who will use it.
The building is a shell wrapped around the actions of the people called
forth by their common faith." [1]
—*The Reverend James L. Doom*

With rare exceptions, history has judged church buildings to be
exceptionally good architecture when they faithfully reflected
the beliefs, traditions, and actions of the people who used them. Although we cannot satisfy today's demands by copying past models, history can help us by providing information as to how Christians of other
times created building forms to meet their needs. It should not be forgotten, however, that the great churches of history were themselves
contemporary to the time in which they were built.

In ancient pagan worship the god was almost always thought to be
located in a sacred place, such as a mountain, a river, a cave. Only
priests were permitted to enter the dwelling of the god and commune

with it. The rest of the community was relegated to a public place separated from the god except for the mediation of the priests.

The absence of an idol or tangible god was one characteristic that distinguished the early Jewish temple from pagan worship, although there were some similarities. For example, the temple of the Jews contained an empty holy place that only priests could enter; the people performed their sacrifices of purification at altars outside the temple. As in pagan worship, they were not permitted to enter the final cell, or holy place, which only the priests could enter.

The temple was not the only place set aside for religious services. In addition, synagogues were developed to provide local places for teaching and worship for Jews in the Diaspora. As the temple was for priests and sacrifices, the synagogue became the place where laymen gathered. Through the synagogues the Jews affirmed that God could not be finally placed or located in one spot, but that He was a spirit who was also present among his people. A desk was placed in the midst of the congregation for the reading of the Scriptures; there was no holy place such as existed in the temple, and there was no privileged priesthood on whom the people depended for communication with God. Worship was relatively free and informal. Any male, for example, could stand up to interpret the Scriptures.

Early Christian Worship

After Pentecost, the Christians did not break with the temple, and continued to attend the synagogues. Hostility, however, soon developed between Christians and Jews, largely as a result of the attempts of the Christians to evangelize both Jews and Gentiles. It was not long before the Christians began to hold most of their meetings in homes that were made available to them. Because of their familiarity with worship in the synagogues, it is not surprising that the style of worship in the synagogue influenced early Christian worship to a remarkable degree.

Many of the homes used by the Christians were of a Roman style built around a courtyard called an *atrium.* Small chambers opened off the atrium, and access to it was from the street through a porch called a *vestibulum.* The atrium was not used for worship except on rare occasions, but the small rooms opening off the atrium were adapted to meet the people's needs.

The traditions of the temple and the synagogue met in the early house church. The early Christians believed that the death and resurrection of Christ rendered the temple ritual meaningless, and therefore they no longer felt compelled to follow the temple traditions of sacrifice. In effect, the service of communion became the substitute for the ancient temple rites, although the concept of sacrifice was carried forward in Christian worship, as was the liturgical use of the Psalter. The early Christians continued the practice of reading and meditating on God's word and the custom of corporate prayer which they had inherited from the synagogue. Thus the worship life of the church became centered in these two essential actions: the study and proclamation of God's word and the observance of the Lord's Supper, or, as it came to be called, the Eucharist.

The persecution of the first three centuries was not so continuous as is commonly assumed, and worship was not always limited to the secrecy of the catacombs and other hiding places. Before the fourth century, in both the eastern and western segments of the Roman Empire and beyond its borders, Christians no longer met exclusively in private houses, and large buildings were constructed especially for that purpose. Very often these buildings were inspired by the civic basilica, which was the style of one of the most prevalent Roman public buildings of that day.

The persecutions did have one result that played a very important role in the development of worship. Many early Christians died as martyrs, and since it was assumed that martyrs were unusually close to Christ, the early Christians found comfort in venerating their physical remains. Whenever possible, altars were built in the tombs of those saints. The ancient pagan quest to localize a god prevailed once again as the altars took on special characteristics. New types of sanctuaries or chapels, called *martyria,* were erected to house these altars. Many of these were circular or polygonal in shape, and in time they became centered on a coffin-altar. Most of the actions of worship were performed on the coffin-altar, which was deemed peculiarly sacred. Some of the consequences of localizing God in this fashion are evident even today.

The viewpoint of the early church on art was frequently one of opposition to the religious use of pictures and other visual arts. This position was based apparently on religious grounds and was undoubtedly derived from the Jewish traditions and prohibitions against idolatry.

The expectation that Christ would soon return must also have made such artistic efforts appear futile and irrelevant. At any rate, there are few if any surviving examples of Christian art forms that can be dated safely before the third century.

The pictures drawn on the walls of the catacombs are probably the first expressions of Christian art. Here we can still see drawings and symbols that were used not only as a means of primitive communication, but also to express a faith that was the source of their courage. Although there is no evidence that the early Christians used carvings or paintings as objects of worship, probably the simple and obviously nonidolatrous nature of the art they developed in the catacombs prepared the way for a more general acceptance of art in church buildings erected after Constantine's time.

There have been many attempts to draw guidelines from the early Church that would be helpful today in the renewal of Christian worship, and from time to time it is suggested that the kind of buildings used then make clear what ought to be done today. While there are insights to be learned from the manner in which the early Christians worshiped and lived, it does not follow that the buildings they used for meeting places are adequate models for what is needed today.

On the other hand, there is a lesson in the way the early Christians went about their tasks. They did not waste time with undue concern for the kinds of buildings they were using, but seized upon those building forms that were available and contemporary. They were not interested in creating monuments but were primarily concerned with erecting buildings that would serve as places for the community of faith to gather and carry out its tasks. Today we could become much more effective if we displayed the same sense of urgency in discharging our responsibilities as Christians.

The Church Adopts the Basilica

When the persecutions ceased in the fourth century, the Emperor Constantine encouraged the building of a number of churches. As crowds began to attend the churches in ever larger numbers, the clergy monopolized many of the acts of worship that had been the responsibility and privilege of those who participated in the services during the days of persecution. Almost inevitably, an earlier intimacy was lost, and worship increasingly reflected the splendor of Rome.

The basilica became the architectural answer for the church building needs of this period. The civil basilica of the Roman Empire, which served many public purposes from courthouse to stock exchange, was usually oblong in shape and divided by colonnades which supported the roof; at the very end of the building—or occasionally on one side —there was a recessed, semicircular alcove called an apse. In the civil buildings, the magistrate and his assistants sat in the apse on benches against the curved wall, and the church easily adapted this form to its own purposes, placing the bishop at the center of the apse in the same place reserved for the magistrate. The curve of the apse on either side of the bishop's seat contained seats for the presbyters (ministers). The altar stood on the chord of the apse and, after the fifth century, was frequently used as a repository for the relics of saints. A canopy was sometimes erected over the altar. While the altar still had some of the characteristics of a table, it was increasingly considered a place of veneration. The platform of the apse was usually extended into the nave and reserved solely for the use of the clergy. The Scriptures were read from the ambo, a pulpitlike reading desk that was constructed as a further extension of the chancel platform. The sermon was probably preached from the bishop's throne. The space directly in front of the altar/table was often occupied by the lesser clergy, or by singers.

As the Western church continued to use the basilican form, the buildings became longer, thus reflecting the increased emphasis on ritual acts performed by the clergy in behalf of the gathered community. Despite this tendency and the increasing separation of clergy from the people, the principal idea of worship in the basilica remained that of both Word—emphasized by the central bishop's throne—and sacrament, symbolized by the central altar/table. Notwithstanding, it is easy to see the beginnings of medieval worship patterns in the lengthened basilicas, the choirs reserved for the clergy, and the apse, with its emphasis on the priests gathered around the sacred, canopied altar.

In those countries bordering the eastern Mediterranean—in the Eastern church, that is—church buildings developed differently. It became the custom to dedicate each church in honor of the saint whose remains were enshrined within. Eastern churches became essentially tombs that were also used for worship. The architectural solution for these churches was the square, polygonal, or circular building, usually capped by a dome. This style was preserved throughout the Byzantine era, and in time it crossed the Mediterranean to Italy and beyond.

The Middle Ages and Gothic Architecture

As the Christian world entered the Middle Ages, worship underwent a profound change. More and more, the people were merely observers, and the clergy's role took on increasing importance. Changes in the design of the church buildings were not long in coming, and by the end of the twelfth century a new style, which was remarkably well suited to medieval theology and worship, had come into acceptance. In time this design was given the name of "Gothic."

Even today Gothic churches are marvels of construction and engineering, and their steep pitched roofs, graceful arches, and flying buttresses still excite wonder and admiration. Gothic church buildings, all of great height, were necessarily narrow because of the engineering requirements imposed by the vaulted roof. In order to accommodate large crowds and to harmonize aesthetically with the height of the vault, they also had to be long.

Typically, at least half of the building was devoted to the chancel. Usually a screen was erected that separated the nave from the chancel and the laity from the clergy. Commonly called the "rood screen," because of the large cross (rood) that often surrounded it, this was usually solid in monastic and cathedral churches, but in parish churches it was more often of wooden tracery that permitted the people to glimpse the liturgical action within the chancel. The pulpit was generally positioned at the side of the nave outside the chancel and was the place the priest used on occasion to address the people.

The development of the long chancel resulted in large part from its constant use by the religious and the clergy in saying the daily office. In fact, church law decreed that the chancel must be treated as a separate building from the nave, which was used by the laity for their worship—and that usually only on Sunday mass. Lay patrons were often given stalls inside the chancel, but for most others, the chancel was "off limits," except, of course, to monks and the clergy. A few singers may have occupied some of the stalls, but they were usually in a loft erected over the rood screen. After the rebuilding of Canterbury Cathedral in the twelfth century, however, it became customary to place the monastic choir within the chancel. Thus the established plan for build-ing cathedrals essentially divided the building into three parts: the nave (where the people stood), the choir, and the sanctuary (the space about the altar which was reserved for the priests). The people were barred from both choir and altar by the screen.

In setting the clergy apart as a privileged class, the Gothic cathedral reflected the age perfectly. It was sympathetic to a theological belief that man was helpless without the mediation of clergy and church. It emphasized the awesomeness of God. It symbolized the church's role as the world's most powerful institution, and implied that worship was not an act in which each individual was to be personally involved. Church building committees should have some understanding of the role the Gothic church actually played in the medieval church, since there is a great deal of romanticized sentiment that still sees these struc-tures as a "more Christian" type of building that should be the goal of every church. While the Gothic building served medieval worship practices very well, it is difficult to see how it is compatible with con-temporary concepts of Christian worship, whether Protestant or Cath-olic. To build a Gothic structure as an example of Christian architec-ture today would be to suggest that the church is committed to medieval assumptions about theology and worship, or is unconcerned as to whether its buildings reflect its true belief.

The Renaissance and the Reformation

With the Renaissance, the "otherworldliness" of the Middle Ages gave way to a new humanism and concern for the natural world, a contrast that can be seen clearly in a comparison of the art of the different periods. Where previously the church had been the exclusive patron of artists and had dictated a limited range of subject matter, the art of the Renaissance reveals a great enthusiasm for a vast variety of nonreligious subjects.

The growing concern for the individual which characterized much of the Renaissance undoubtedly prepared the way for the Reformation and the birth of Protestantism. After the events which culminated in the break with Rome, the reformers faced many needs, but these did not include new church buildings. Except for necessity, the reformers simply used the structures they had inherited. People had been accustomed to the existing buildings, and there appeared to be no obvious reason for radical change. With the exception of some of the Lutheran churches, a number of changes were frequently made that did not require major renovations. The pulpit was given a new emphasis as a liturgical center. Pulpit ornamentation, statuary, and stained-glass windows were removed as the reformers attempted to rid themselves of things they considered idolatrous. The screen separating nave and chancel was sometimes retained, but in those cases the church was treated as two separate rooms: the whole congregation would, on occasion, move into the chancel for the celebration of communion while continuing to meet in the separated nave for other services. Thus the screen divided the church but did not divide congregation from clergy.

In other churches the old chancel was practically abandoned. There was considerable experimentation with the location of the holy table, varying from the placing of a small table near the pulpit to having long tables in the nave at which the congregation sat for the celebration of the Lord's Supper.

While there was no common pattern in the new churches, in most cases it is evident that a conscious effort was made to have the liturgical arrangement of the building be an accurate reflection of Reformation belief. Since the various Protestant churches developed with differing traditions, there were many kinds of church buildings erected. At least two kinds of architecture should be mentioned, however, as having special influence: the Anglican churches designed by Christopher Wren and the churches built in the tradition of the Puritans.

Architecture of Christopher Wren

The Great Fire of 1666 in London set the stage for a church-building boom that in many ways was unparalleled until World War II recreated some of the same conditions. A major portion of the city was destroyed, including eighty-four of the city's churches, and Sir Christopher Wren (1632–1723) was selected as the architect to design new buildings for fifty-two of them. Wren saw this task as something more than replacing destroyed churches, and he proceeded to develop a fresh style of building that had a lasting effect on ecclesiastical architecture in Europe and the United States.

Wren's best-known church is St. Paul's, but it was in the parish churches of London that he showed his greatest creativity. His success in large measure is the result of his understanding of Protestant church worship. He was obviously sensitive to the liturgical principles that had been developed over the previous century and set forth in the Book of Common Prayer. One of his principal concerns was that all persons who worshiped in his churches should be able to hear and see, and to achieve this goal he even computed how close a person had to be to the pulpit in order to hear distinctly. He described his buildings as "auditories," thus distinguishing them from the Roman Catholic churches of that time in which the people could see the elevated host but could not understand what was being said.

The churches designed by Wren show sensitivity to the needs of the congregation. An adequate pulpit was always provided, and in some churches the reading desk and pulpit were combined with a clerk's seat to form a three-decker pulpit. This combination of pulpit, reading desk, and clerk's seat dramatized the unity of worship by making it possible to conduct most of the services from one liturgical center.

Because of the traditions of that day,[2] it was necessary for Wren to provide in each church an altar that was positioned against the wall of the church and set off by a railing. In most cases this was done without simulating a chancel. Pulpit, reading desk, and clerk's pew were placed closer to the congregation, either combined or placed on either side of the central aisle. The font usually remained near the main entrance. The congregation was seated in high box pews on the floor of the nave or in the gallery as close as possible to the two main liturgical centers: altar and pulpit-reading desk. The building was always capped by a steeple, and the style and beauty of Wren's steeples became the model for church steeples in England and the United States for many years.

Wren's church plan set the style for Anglican churches until the 1840s. They were one-room buildings without chancels, featuring a three-decker pulpit designed so people could see and hear all that transpired. Only the baptismal font remained in the rear of the church, situated in its medieval position.

During the rebuilding of London following the Great Fire, many Anglican churches used the former Puritan preaching halls as temporary places in which to meet. Some have suggested that this experience kindled a new interest in preaching, with the result that Wren was prodded by many of his clients to design a building that took preaching seriously. Whether or not this is true, there are points of similarity between the buildings erected for Puritan worship and the Wren churches. Both were auditory, and put their principal emphasis on preaching. Bringing worshipers as close to the centers of worship as possible, both were direct and straightforward in their design.

Puritan Meetinghouses

The Wren churches differed from the Puritan meetinghouses of London principally in the slightly greater prominence given the altar/ table and in the fine organ cases, which were normally placed in the rear of the building over the entrance. The Wren churches were also more richly decorated, but this "difference" was probably in great part the result of having more money to spend than the Puritans!

In the Puritan churches, the entire service was led from the pulpit except during the receiving of the sacraments. Pulpits often were extremely large, sometimes reaching higher than ten feet. Many were aesthetic triumphs, with curved stairways and impressive sounding boards above. Galleries were quite common, and, consequently, a large number of people could be seated close to the pulpit. The table was placed in front of the pulpit and, when needed, a baptismal basin was placed upon it. The Puritan buildings aimed at simplicity, reflected in the pews, pulpit, and the use of a plain table. These meetinghouses, as one historian wrote, were "elegant in their simplicity. There were no traditional ecclesiastical symbols but there was a directness in building for a specific type of worship. . . . For their purposes they were wonderfully successful examples of liturgical architecture." [3]

The colonists brought the New England meetinghouse to this country, where it went through several stages of evolution. The earliest, most primitive examples often served as forts against Indian attacks as well as places of worship. In the eighteenth century these buildings were replaced by larger ones that were almost square, with the pulpit placed opposite the main door in the center of the wall. After 1700 these churches became more complex in design, with more elaborate woodwork in portions of the interior. Brick was occasionally substituted for wood, and steeples and towers began to reflect the influence of Wren. The buildings became slightly rectangular, with the pulpit in the center of one of the long sides. Nevertheless, they almost always maintained their essential character as meetinghouses where the Word of God was preached.

After the Revolutionary War, a new type of meetinghouse emerged, with the pulpit located in the center of one of the narrow sides. A narthex, or entryway, was added to the building. Even then there was no suggestion of a chancel, and since choirs and organs were practically unknown in those churches, no provision was made for singers. In the nineteenth and twentieth centuries, however, many of these churches were "chancelized" in a frustrated search for romantic or medieval forms that would also solve "the choir problem"!

Puritan architecture played a substantial role in the early architecture not only of the Congregational churches but also those of the other denominations that are the descendants of the nonconformist movement. The buildings that Presbyterians, Baptists, and other independents erected were also plain and unadorned, designed to hear the Word of God and to encourage worship in accordance with their firmly held beliefs.

The story of Methodism is different. Starting as a movement within the Church of England, its initial services were intended as a supplement, not a substitute, for Anglican worship. The early Methodist buildings were referred to as "preaching houses," with Anglican churches continuing to administer the sacraments. In time the sacraments were also administered in the preaching houses, and it became customary to build an altar with a rail around it so that the communicants could receive the elements while kneeling, in the same fashion as in the Anglican churches of that day. Since most of the Methodists were poor, the chapels were usually simple and contained no decorations. Early Methodist chapels resembled the meeting places of the nonconformists, with the exception of the altar and rail.

Nineteenth-Century "Styles"

The experimentation that characterized most of the previous two hundred years came to a halt in the nineteenth century. Some denominations, particularly those which did not trace their heritage from Calvin, turned to the forms of previous centuries; no building was considered "Christian" unless it imitated the cathedrals of the Middle Ages. At the same time, other churches were building auditoriums, with no concern for aesthetics. These churches served not only as centers for preaching, but also as places where sinners were exhorted to repent and be saved. The pulpit shrank in size, while the platform reached mammoth proportions in order to accommodate large choirs and the frenetic movements of preachers exhorting their audiences to seek forgiveness.

Auditorium-type buildings were the result of the revival movement within Protestantism, with its emphasis on individual conversion. Many now appear grotesque, and much of the church-building boom since World War II has been directed toward their replacement. The exteriors of these churches often presented fascinating contradictions to their interiors. The exterior might be Georgian or classical, but the interior was invariably cold and, to contemporary taste, almost ugly.

A much-maligned model of about 1900 was the Akron plan, so called because of its origin in a building erected in Akron, Ohio. The Akron plan was basically a long rectangular room divided by a movable partition into worship and Sunday school sections. The partition could on occasion be raised to accommodate large crowds. The pulpit was placed in one corner, with the choir in back and a small table in front. The floor sloped toward the pulpit, with the congregation gathered about the pulpit in curved pews. The Sunday school section was used for assembly, after which the students would meet in adjoining classrooms.

In fact, the Akron plan was a remarkable representation of beliefs and practices that were then contemporary. The Akron plan was widely copied, but educational and theological concepts underwent a rapid change, and many churches later found themselves saddled with obsolete buildings.

The Akron plan has long been superseded by new approaches to Christian education that place the church school in separate rooms and buildings, but those who criticize it would be well advised to take a good look at today's changing demands in the light of the great sums spent on church-school facilities. It is possible that the mistakes of the past are being repeated and that many of our expensive and elaborate education buildings may become obsolete more quickly than anticipated.

Revivalist individualism and Gothic romanticism joined forces prior to World War II to create a generation of mongrel buildings. The individualism of the revival churches gave way to more sophisticated emotions that found the "worshipful atmosphere" of Gothic buildings very compatible. The split chancel was seen as the ideal location for the choir, which preferred to sing at or to a congregation rather than with it. The rheostat provided the necessary lighting to induce the right mood, and it was not long before Congregationalists, Presbyterians, Methodists, and Anglicans were building churches that all looked alike in their imitation of medieval styles.

Revival hymns began to swell in pseudo-Gothic settings; the New England meetinghouses were even remodeled with divided chancels so that they might become "more worshipful"; and new Georgian Colonials were erected with the finest attention to detail but with a split chancel that would have shocked any churchman at the time of the American Revolution!

The "Modern" Movement

It was not long before this architectural hodgepodge began to receive penetrating criticisms. In addition to the rising costs of construction accompanying World War II, making a re-creation of the Middle Ages impossible, questions were asked concerning the appropriate role of the clergy in worship, the relative importance of the sacraments, the involvement of the laity in the corporate act of worship, and the relationship of building to mission. It was within this context that the liturgical renewal had its beginning, and the possibility of a genuinely contemporary American church architecture emerged.

Probably the most significant breakthrough came when artists, architects, and churchmen realized the simple truth—that all the great architectural forms of the past had been contemporary expressions of the beliefs and liturgical practices of each age. As soon as churches sought to design buildings that reflected their belief they were once again asking the right questions and seeking the right answers.

In addition, the revolution in building materials has added new possibilities to all architecture. The modern movement is less than fifty years old, but it has shown an amazing ability to create varied forms that could not previously have been built. Critics often date contemporary church architecture from Notre-Dame du Raincy, a church built in 1923 in a small community east of Paris. August Perret (1874–1954), the architect, made a radical break with all previous church building by using reinforced concrete throughout. Concrete supporting columns and panel walls of concrete, which were prefabricated and pierced with openings filled with colored glass, create an atmosphere reminiscent of some of the European cathedrals, but also make clear that the building is thoroughly contemporary.

Since then the modern movement has developed in many directions, sometimes without much discipline. Modern churches often betray the same lack of concern for fundamentals that pseudo-Gothic buildings did fifty years ago. In Europe, however, the liturgical renewal, the discovery of new building materials and techniques, the need for new construction following World War II, and the receptivity of architects and churchmen to new design possibilities have united to create some of the clearest and freshest churches in the last century. Needless to say, not all these European experiments have been successful, but they are imaginative in concept and elegant in their restraint, simplicity, and directness.

These European churches should not be seen as prototypes to be re-created with American trappings, but should be studied for their inherent taste and as examples of the power of understatement. Seen as departure points rather than styles to copy, they constitute a major challenge to American creativity. The danger is that churches will try to solve their building problems by deciding to put up a "modern" building that is superficial in concept. Modernity in itself settles nothing; church architecture must always begin with the essential questions: For what purposes is the building to be used? What kind of community gathers there? What, really, is the church for?

---✦ ✳ ✦---

CHAPTER FOUR

Of Art and Symbols

"If you are going to build a church you are going to create a thing which speaks. It will speak of meanings, and of values, and it will go on speaking. And if it speaks of the wrong values it will go on destroying." [1]
—*Robert Maguire*

To build a church is to possess the opportunity—and the obligation—to create a work of art.

Many Protestants have always had difficulty understanding and accepting art as a valid expression of religious men. Paul Tillich has commented that from its very beginning "the Protestant faith has been at odds with the visual artes, including church architecture," and that the "predominance of the 'ear' over and against the 'eye' in Protestant thought resulted in Protestantism creating great music and great poetry, but not great architecture, painting, and sculpture." [2]

While some have claimed that this estrangement is the result of the Puritan influence, sterility in art forms has not been limited to this tradition. Neither is this problem entirely a Protestant one, for the Roman Catholic Church, particularly in America, has created its share of ugly and mediocre art. The fact is that art and the church have not been on satisfactory terms for years, and that, while both have suffered from this, the church has been the greater loser.

One art historian, Thomas F. Mathews, S.J., argues that religious "commissions have contributed next to nothing to modern art, or for that matter to the modern religious experience. They are mongrel curiosities without significance and without sequel." [3] Undoubtedly many would disagree, but any objective survey of contemporary art is forced to conclude that few artists have demonstrably drawn their inspiration from traditional Christianity.

The insights, aspirations, and inspiration of artists are badly needed, but the church finds it difficult to accept the work of those who no longer profess loyalty to Christianity. The fact remains that some of our most sensitive art forms are the work of artists who do not claim a formal relationship to Christianity, and in some cases even question the relevance of many traditional beliefs. Marshall McLuhan has observed that artists are perhaps the only persons who are truly sensitive to the present and the future; if so, the church would be well advised to re-establish communication for its own enlightenment and not cavalierly reject the work of those who question and express personal doubts and reservations.

To bridge the gap that now exists, churches should be prepared to take the initiative and commission works from capable and sensitive artists, and be generous in the compensation and latitude given them. Some of the things these artists may wish to portray will clash with our traditional understanding of "religious art," but, although there is no reason to use a statement that contradicts the Gospel in its essentials, churches must be careful not to discard a work of art on the basis of a superficial judgment as to its "Christian" content. A commissioned work should be accepted unless competent critics believe it is clearly inconsistent with basic Christianity. It is time for the church to prove that it can once again be a patron of the arts.

But are we of the institutional church prepared to do this?

It is interesting to speculate on how many church building committees would judge Barnett Newman's "Stations of the Cross" as acceptable for their buildings. The objections would probably not be based on the assumption that the paintings are appropriate only to the Roman Catholic Church; rather, the objections would focus on a so-called "lack of content." Newman has not portrayed the Stations in literal terms, as his vocabulary consists of filling large canvases with a single color, interrupted only occasionally by vertical stripes. Father Mathews, in commenting on the work, describes Newman's art in this manner:

He [Newman] rejected the concept of easel painting by enlarging the canvas beyond the dimensions which the eye can comprehend from the normal distance. This does not imply that one is supposed to step back; the painting is meant to engulf the spectator. . . . Newman has rejected all the preoccupations of the European painters with formal structures. In Newman there is no framing, no balance, no geometry, no ornament, indeed no image.[4]

Mathews concludes that the "Stations" do indeed have religious meaning, and suggests that the true meaning of the terrible walk up the Via Dolorosa can best be described in this manner rather than in more traditional and literal portrayals. But would most building committees agree? We would no doubt be tempted to question whether these masterpieces are really "religious." And yet it is this very failure to question our presuppositions that has caused the church to judge inadmissible much of the work of today's artists.

In one sense, everything in a good church building should be a work of art. The design of the communion table, the pulpit, pews, windows, organ, place for the choir—indeed its total architectural statement—should reveal artistic sensitivity.

But on what basis should art do more than quietly validate the architectural design of the structure as a place that is aesthetically satisfying? The typical Protestant answers to such a question frequently imply disapproval of all art that is not literal and pictorial in character.

"Religious" Pictorial Art

Pictorial art—that is, art which resembles a photograph of a person, event, or thing—has a legitimate role, but "religious" pictorial art is almost always bad. The artistic fundamentalism that sponsors it is usually unresponsive to the evocative and symbolic aspects of art, preferring a highly sentimental experience that glosses over life's realities.

The results can be seen in both Catholic and Protestant churches in the United States. The statuary that clutters many Roman Catholic churches is only slightly more literal than the various representational paintings that Protestants, even today, delight in hanging in the pastor's study, the narthex, on and over the table and pulpit, and in each church-school classroom. The "Jesus pictures" of the last twenty-five years are only one example of this pictorial art, in which poor taste vies with theological ignorance. In despair over the repeated demands of laymen for pictures that "tell the biblical story," architects and some artists have moved to the extremity of starkness and barrenness, leaving many to conclude that art can serve no responsible purpose in worship.

It is almost as if the Christian patron is suspicious of any work of art not immediately transparent to every viewer. Contemporary forms are rejected because we do not understand the artist's meaning, failing to realize that the ultimate question is what the work of art means to us. Even great representational works are not great because of what the artist intended but by reason of the responses they call forth in those who view them. The literal qualities of a Pieta by Michelangelo do not make it a masterpiece so much as the elements of mystery and abstraction that move the viewer to respond with deep emotion and understanding to an intangible quality that haunts the work as a whole.

The difficulty with much pictorial art is that it induces an easy acceptance that approves the work without significant personal involvement. We can view it with complete detachment; it is unnecessary to invest any part of ourselves to see and understand it, and then go on our way. Compare this kind of experience with that described by Mark Rothko, certainly no literalist, but one of the great artists of our time. Rothko claims that he is not interested in relationships of color or form, but is "interested only in expressing basic human emotions— . . . tragedy, ecstasy, doom, and so on. The people who weep before my pictures are having the same religious experience I had when I painted them. And if you . . . are moved only by their color relationships, then you miss the point." [5] Ask yourself when you were last moved significantly by a literal picture of an event that happened long ago.

The failure of pictorial art to involve the viewer in a significant manner has led some to conclude that the only art that has profound religious meaning today is necessarily abstract in character. Such art at least requires the viewer to probe beneath the obvious, and frequently results in a heightened sensitivity. It has the capacity to stir responses that are parallel to those occasioned by faith. It is often "religious" in the profoundest sense of the word.

Decoration and Other Art Forms

Most purists would argue that true art cannot perform a decorative function and that nothing can truly be art unless it can stand on its own, more or less independent of the environment in which it is placed. Such a position can perhaps be sustained from a critic's point of view, but the question remains: What forms of decoration are appropriate for an environment in which people will work and worship?

Church buildings require an appropriate décor which is artistically created and arranged. Objects that serve this purpose must be characterized by restraint and by the manner in which they are subordinated to the tone of the entire building. Ideally, art of this kind is so unobtrusive that most persons entering the building will not be aware of individual objects, or aware even that art has been used for decorative purposes. By its definition, decorative art should not be overtly used to enhance the beauty of places which are the centers of congregational attention, such as the communion table. Good taste, restraint, subordination to the character of the whole—these are the guidelines which should indicate whether a particular form of art is appropriate to the occasion.

Stained or colored glass is another form of art that has been scorned in many "contemporary" church buildings. Such an attitude on the part of architects and building committees may be a serious oversight, as color is not incompatible with contemporary buildings. In fact, one of the most famous recent examples of religious architecture, Le Corbusier's chapel at Ronchamp, France, has been widely praised for the chunks of colored glass interspersed throughout one wall in a fascinating, irregular design.

At the same time, we need to remember that art can be used for some purposes that are antithetical to the church. In an age of affluence, the commissioning and ownership of works of art has become a status symbol, and churches have sometimes acquired art in an attempt to be fashionable. The accumulation of miscellaneous art for purposes of advertising wealth and position is not consistent with Christian mission. Art can be used cheaply, carelessly, or thoughtlessly, on the one hand, while for some sophisticates it can even become a substitute for religion.

Because art has such a varied potential for good and bad, the process by which it is selected and commissioned is extremely important. Here the architect can play a major role. His training and experience should make him thoroughly grounded in the qualities of good art, and his judgment should be given special consideration by the building committee. The latter rarely possesses the background to select and commission art; its most effective work can be performed by providing the artist with a statement of the church's theological principles and then trusting both artist and architect to interpret these principles faithfully.

Preconditioned by years of having the "fine arts" presented in a museum atmosphere rather than in the everyday world, some of us find it difficult to appreciate architecture as an art form. While decorative art may be properly used in a church, good architecture does not mean a building known primarily for its embellishments. A building that is good art possesses an integrity of its own which can only be cheapened by extravagant decoration. Rather than encourage exercises in architectural self-indulgence, we might look again at Quaker meetinghouses; their simplicity often encompasses all the factors that constitute good art.

Guidelines for Appreciating Contemporary Art

Many of us are inhibited from commissioning present-day artists because of an inability to understand and appreciate the idiom, themes, and purposes of modern art. Because of our familiarity with art that simply reproduces a scene or picture, we are often blind to the potentiality of abstract and other forms of nonrepresentational art. Although this is not the place for a detailed explanation on how we can become more sensitive to contemporary experiments, several guidelines may be helpful:

—In viewing what is broadly called "modern art," it is not necessary to discern the artist's intention in a canvas, sculpture, or other medium. In a very real sense, art involves communication in several dimensions. The artist may have one basis of communication with his work, but his intention and personal beliefs are not the critical concerns of the observer. The important question is: What response does the art object evoke from those who view it?

This response may be quite different from that of the artist, but in a sense the artist is finished with the work, and the only living communication is that which exists between the art object and the viewer.

—Do not always seek to find meaning in nonrepresentational art. Even if it merely contributes to an environmental effect, this does not mean it is an unsuccessful work of art.

—Do not think of "content" in terms of reminders of familiar objects. The challenge of the new can itself be the very meaning of the art object.

—Art created for the church need not suggest a specific "religious" concept. The quality of the work, the implications of its content, the environment in which it is set may all combine to evoke a response that is more profoundly religious than the comfortable memories called forth by a conventional picture of pious events.

Symbols

While art has a symbolic dimension, symbols are often simply common objects that have taken on special meanings. The cross itself is an example of this.

Symbols are self-authenticating, that is, the symbol itself is a vehicle of communication and does not require extensive interpretation. Its purpose is justified by the response it calls forth from people. When it fails to evoke a meaningful response, it can no longer be considered an effective symbol.

Symbolic value is sometimes assigned to objects that are thought to have special meaning, but this meaning may have been lost in time. To say that a tree is the symbol of life, a lamb stands for Christ, the dove for purity and peace, and ivy for death and immortality may be misleading, since people today cannot be expected to make such translations whenever these objects appear on church walls or in stained-glass windows. Unfortunately, these objects do not retain their erstwhile power of evocation, and only an extraordinarily creative artist could employ them with conviction today.

For an object to remain a symbol, it must retain the power to evoke response or emotion in a substantial number of those who encounter it. Although once considered symbols, objects which no longer have this capacity are in fact clichés that are either meaningless signs or a means whereby people can sentimentally relive past events.

Symbols cannot be created from information in reference books or requisitioned through a mail-order catalog. Symbols are necessary to the religious life of men, but they must grow out of experiences that are related to human emotions. The question, therefore, is not "What objects are good symbols to put in our church?" but rather "What objects have special meaning to us as a people of faith?"

Paul Tillich has described this as an age of broken symbols, and there may be few objects left that have the capacity for broad communication. Stanley VanDerBeek, the experimental film producer, has suggested that lasting symbols are no longer possible in a culture of instant communication, high mobility, and rapidly changing values. To him the only symbols that are meaningful are those that serve an immediate purpose and are then abandoned—such as those created by motion pictures. Sister Mary Corita has stated with her pop art that the important symbols of our times are those one finds in magazines, on billboards, and in such items as bread wrappers and labels for canned food. In one of her major exhibits, all of her posters and statements were pasted on hundreds of cardboard boxes, as if to say that the exhibit has value for today, but tomorrow's needs will require something else. These apostles of the transient symbol are in rebellion against our religious clichés, and suggest that it is better to confess the symbolic poverty of our times than invent new symbols which are meant to have a permanent quality but, in fact, quickly reveal their contrived nature.

Those who would write off the potential of symbols in an age such as this should study the success many commercial organizations enjoy by using objects as a means of communication in advertising. This should indicate that religious symbols are not impossible, but require a continual updating. Many traditional objects still fulfill the requirements of a religious symbol—the open Book, the tablets of the Law, the chalice, and, as has been suggested, the cross. In order to create new symbols, it may be helpful to examine how many of our outdated symbols evolved from the symbolic language of the Scriptures—the vine, the tree of life, etc. Today we have a new vocabulary which gives symbolic meaning to words such as ecumenism, humanization, involvement, and even communication. Therefore, the task is to bring these new verbal symbols into objective reality and relevance instead of using the signs of the dead past.

Architecture itself can be a symbol if its form and the enclosed space evoke significant responses. Many Gothic cathedrals still stir people deeply, and the best of our contemporary buildings possess the same quality. The pilgrimage chapel at Ronchamp, France, for example, whatever its limitations as a functioning church, demonstrates Le Corbusier's genius because its symbolic, sculpted form involves people in an unforgettable emotional experience.

"Looking Like a Church"

Great architecture speaks with eloquence, but churches must ask whether it also speaks of the right values. The form and quality of the building should be consistent with the Gospel the church wishes to proclaim. For example, it should not be designed to generate awe at the expense of all other religious emotions. Awe may be a part of worship, but it is also important for people to worship through praise, thanksgiving, and celebration. If a building is overwhelming in its suggestion of the majesty of God, it may become impossible for a person to break through this barrier and see his relationship to God in its fullest dimensions. A building is obviously a failure as church architecture if it inhibits those who worship there.

When church building committees are asked to prepare a statement of those qualities which should be represented by the shape of the building and the space enclosed within it, they usually respond by pleading that it should be a "church that looks like a church." Some people may regard such expectations as unsophisticated, but there is need for churches that look like churches, if this phrase is correctly understood.

A congregation has the right to expect that its new building will not be easily confused with those erected for other purposes. It should also expect that its building will function adequately by providing an appropriate environment for its members to gather in worship and work.

On the other hand, too many building committees that cry for "a church that looks like a church" are actually more interested in erecting an imposing billboard that will advertise to the town that this is a church which "fits" into the community. Such people are not looking for church architecture but simply trying to fulfill some romanticized idea of the visual appearance of a church.

Architectural Clichés

Even a little knowledge of history helps us see how in church architecture, as in other areas, today's innovation becomes tomorrow's convention. The New England meetinghouse was a practical solution for the needs of its day, but it was not long before this form became the norm that could not be varied. A more recent example is the "A-frame chapel." Mr. Warren Weber, AIA, of Portland, Oregon, is credited (or blamed) for the design of the first so-called "teepee" church, a chapel for the then new Community Church at Cedar Hills, Oregon. Its steeply pitched roof-to-the-ground motif was an architectural answer to a very limited building budget for a mission church. Although besieged by requests from all over the country for copies of the working drawings for the building, Mr. Weber has steadfastly refused to provide them, and in fact has never designed another "teepee" chapel. Unfortunately, this has not deterred building committees or architects; the Cedar Hills chapel has been turned into a stereotype and can be seen duplicated almost to the smallest detail in practically every state.

The A-frame chapel and the New England meetinghouse are but two examples of forms that have taken on "sacred" characteristics and now represent to many "what a church should look like." To dub one form of church architecture as "more like a church" than another is reminiscent of the same kind of rationalization that entrapped the Gothic revivalists of the nineteenth century.

Sometimes churches seem to symbolize Christianity by means of a particular form. One building may resemble a fish; another may look like praying hands, or be shaped like a flower, an anchor, or even a bird. Such self-conscious efforts to express the church's faith usually produce superficial buildings. Such buildings are not designed to help the church be a church but are mere studies in composition and sculpture. The building committee should also recognize the temptation of a congregation to advertise itself as "different" because of the unusual form of its building. This suggests a claim to sophistication and emancipation that is often not valid.

We may conclude that a church which becomes preoccupied with its own community image, whether in the form of a sentimental church building or a daring extravaganza, is proceeding on the wrong track. Architecture is more than an advertising slogan or a bait for the curious; architecture is an art that provides an environment for people who come together to share their faith. A building genuinely reflecting that faith and aesthetically and functionally providing the environment within which its faith can be made manifest will also be architecture that symbolically proclaims the faith to the community.

—◦⊰ ✳ ⊱◦—

PART TWO

Architect,
Building Committee,
Site, and Master Plan:
Critical Concerns
for the Building
Enterprise

The quality of church building as architecture
is determined long before a brick is laid or
any dirt is moved. Its pattern is set by the
creativity of the architect, the quality of the
building committee, the location of the site,
and the preparation of the master plan. These
are the critical concerns that will spell failure
or success for the building enterprise.

—◄❁ ❋ ❁►—

ᴄᴗ4 Key Person:
The ᴗ4rchitect

"Architecture which expresses the kind of integrity which can be
described as religious cannot be accomplished by half-educated,
over-specialized, narrow-minded people. The only hope for success
is in designers who have broad visions and understanding, whose
attitudes and minds are open, curious, visionary, idealistic." [1]
—*E. A. Sövik,* FAIA

The responsibility carried by an architect is vividly illustrated by
William Wenzler, a talented architect in Brookfield, Wisconsin, as
he describes his experience in designing one of his first church buildings. The design concept Wenzler developed included a roof form
which, at that time, had seldom if ever been used in this country.
Usually described as hyperbolic-paraboloid, the roof was to be of thin-
shell concrete, with the weight of the mass resting primarily on two
points. Because of the newness of the design, there was no substantial
body of experience on which Wenzler could rely. Precise engineering
was an obvious necessity, and the best consultative services were employed to help develop the specifications. Thereafter Wenzler submitted his plans to experts in other countries—experts who had had
much experience working with thin-shell concrete—for their counsel and
advice. Their response was simple and to the point: The roof may
stand, but if it does, it will be a coincidence.

Most people of less determination and talent would have abandoned the project, but Wenzler, after carefully reviewing all of his work, concluded that the "experts" were wrong and that his own consultants had indeed provided the correct answer. Unfortunately, in this instance it was not feasible to test the design in model form; the only practical way to proceed was to erect the building, using careful field analysis and taking all possible precautions for safety. This was done; the concrete was poured and then began the period of waiting which must elapse before the forms can be removed. The roof held and the architect's judgment was vindicated. Surely few persons can truly comprehend the implications of the responsibility Wenzler carried alone during those trying weeks.

Mr. Wenzler would be the first to concede that rarely is it possible to erect a building which is perfect in all respects, with no flaw in craftsmanship or design. A building enterprise involves many persons, requires many skills, and can be affected by the decisions and actions of many persons over which the architect has little control. Once the building is erected, the mistakes are there for all to see; often of a permanent character, they cannot be easily glossed over or hidden from public view. The problem is even more complex in the case of church buildings. Many seem to claim a vested interest in the building, and any portion that does not suit their fancy is easily described as a "goof" made by the architect, although he in fact may have been blameless.

Regardless of the flaws which find their way into all buildings, whether designed by an architect or not, the fact remains that if a well-designed and appropriate building is the goal, the architect is a key person. If he is competent, co-operative, and creative, his guidance will result in a quality building of good design that is also capable of meeting the functional requirements of his client.

Qualities Possessed by a Good Architect

It is not easy, however, to find the right architect. The qualities required for high competence in this field are sometimes intangible and often immeasurable: the inspiration the architect's designs suggest, the integrity of his thinking processes, his ability to work with others, his willingness to do needed research to understand fully the needs of his client.

A professional who has spent many years in education and training for his work, a good architect is many things. To begin with, he is a counselor. Much of his time must be devoted to discussions with the church committee on its program requirements. His task demands many skills to bring out the facts and needs upon which he will base his planning.

A good architect is also a designer. He will know and appreciate the importance of design in the ultimate function of the building. He will seek to create a building that is not only a work of art but is also an expression of the church in form and space.

A good architect is a co-ordinator and business administrator. Details do not escape him. He knows the importance of a budget. He recognizes the church as his client and is careful and prudent in handling the affairs entrusted to him.

Finally, a good architect is both advocate and mediator. He accepts the responsibility of seeing that the builder fulfills his contractual commitments to the church. This does not mean he should be legalistic or quick to find fault, but he will realize that honest differences can arise and that it is his responsibility whenever possible to mediate such differences.

This statement was once shown to a contractor who had built several churches. His response was that a better description for a good architect would be hard to imagine, but that the man does not exist who can meet all these requirements!

The contractor, no doubt, reflected his own experiences and prejudices, but he has a point. An architect may not be perfect in all areas and yet he may be the right architect for your church. Balance and judgment are indispensable in measuring any professional talent. The fact that all architects have their strong and weak points does not change the basic fact that the man who is expected to design a church should be a very special person. More is expected and needed from him than from an architect for a commercial building, an industrial facility, or even a home.

Necessity for Employing an Architect

Occasionally, people ask why the church should engage an architect. This query is sometimes prompted by members who suggest that the church try to purchase plans used by some other church, thereby saving "all that money." Or perhaps someone suggests that stock plans can be obtained that will meet the needs of the church. Or a member reports that Mr. Jones has engineering and drawing talents and would be happy to sketch a building that could be built by a contractor friend. Most churches today do not spend too much time considering proposals of this kind, but it is still worth repeating some of the reasons why they should be rejected.

First of all the building of a church is a complex task and does not lend itself easily to patterns that have been used previously. Stock plans are based on the assumption that one church is like every other one, that the site presents the same problems as the next, that each church has the same needs. This is simply not so. Stock plans never really fit a church; all too often they result in poor construction and site development, inadequate space utilization, and stereotyped, sterile architecture. Instead of saving money the church that uses stock plans will be the loser.

Neither should the church rely on the talents of someone who plays at architecture, or an engineer who has not achieved the minimum standards established for professional standing in this special field. There is much more to architecture than drawing handsome renderings, which may be no more than camouflaged disaster. One would not go to an unlicensed lawyer for advice, or to an unlicensed doctor for treatment. Similarly, a church should not spend a great deal of money building a structure that will last for decades without receiving the professional counsel and services of an architect.

Churches are occasionally approached by companies offering a package deal and claiming that the services of a licensed architect are included. Such an architect may be licensed, but rarely is he a member of AIA or any of the other major professional associations. The package usually sets a total cost for the building that includes the architect's fee.

Churches should be cautious about considering such arrangements. It is very easy for the builder to take short cuts in construction that will affect the quality of the building if there is no independent architect responsible for supervision. While not always the case, there is the possibility that the architect has a financial interest in the construction company and thus may reap a double reward as a result of effective sales work and cheapened construction. Another possible problem is that the architect may be inadequately compensated, and, as a result, may be unable to provide a complete architectural service without financial loss. Most companies providing package proposals work from stock plans; thus all the difficulties related to this approach must be considered.

Some churches have been pleased with the work of package companies, but the relative advantages and disadvantages of their proposals should be most carefully analyzed. The building committee should certainly check the quality of work that can be expected by making personal visits to several buildings erected by the company, including jobs completed several years previously, thereby getting a chance to judge the rate of depreciation. Some critics of package programs claim that the product looks good on dedication Sunday, but five years later the doors do not fit, the windows are loose, the flooring is in disrepair, and the building itself looks old long before its time.

Working With Architect—A Learning Process

Working with an architect provides an opportunity for a unique learning process. The architect may learn something from the church, but the church will always learn something from the architect. It can be a very effective kind of Christian education, an experience a church should not miss.

From the first interview, church committees will be engaged in a dialogue that should challenge them to discover what qualities make up architectural excellence. The architect will be able to convey considerable information on the history of ecclesiastical architecture, the structural reasons for various kinds of buildings, and the direction of current architectural thought. This may be a once-in-a-lifetime opportunity to get to know an architect in a professional capacity and share in the creative process. All this is lost when a church turns its problems over to the package dealer, who can all too easily run down a check list and prescribe just the building to fit the church's needs!

Importance of Early Selection

An architect can help a church in many ways if he is employed at a time when he can share in the decision-making processes. For this reason churches should make their selection early, so the architect can share in discussions and make recommendations before final decisions are made.

For too many committees the selection of the architect is seen as the end of their task. Upon signing a contract the committee and the minister give the architect some hastily conceived notions of space needs and tell him to go to work, thereby abdicating their responsibility for the development of a written program. This attitude is encouraged by the rush atmosphere that often prevails in church building programs: the congregation wants to see drawings; the fund-raiser needs a picture for a fund-raising brochure; the finance committee is upset that the bank will not talk in terms of a loan until the church has some drawings. The temptation is to tell the architect to get something out as quickly as possible; if the building program is not complete he can rely on his experience and solve all the program problems for the church.

Sometimes there is a problem because the architect is strong-willed and the building committee indecisive. Committee work requires patience, and an eager architect may well conclude that it is a waste of his time to thresh out the intricate problems of church program planning. For the building committee, there is the temptation to turn all these matters over to the architect. This can have disastrous results. The building may get finished in time, but it may be nothing more than the architect's personal statement, which is not likely to reflect the life, belief, and mission of the church.

The dilemma posed by strong-minded architects and indecisive and impatient committees has led many denominational counselors to recommend that churches put down in writing most of the building program before an architect is engaged. Only in this way can function be clearly delineated and the building committee motivated to do its job in a careful, deliberate, and creative manner. This counsel is born out of frustration, however, and does not describe an ideal arrangement.

Fortunately, architects and churchmen are becoming much more sensitive to their respective roles in planning church buildings. There is a growing feeling that the risks involved in employing an architect early in the planning process are outweighed by the possibilities for learning and inspiration that can come through a continuous, patient, and probing dialogue. Of course, there will be much fruitless talk, but there is great value in the architect and the church getting to know each other well. This is the ideal way for an architect to develop the deep understanding of his client that will help him design the kind of building that will most faithfully serve and symbolize his client's faith. This is not an easy process; it requires the continued contact of persons who seek a common goal and are not satisfied with quick answers.

If the architect respects the integrity of the committee, if the latter continues to function as an indispensable part of the creative process, if each is patient with the other and respects the other's responsibilities and abilities, then the earlier the architect is employed the better.

There are other advantages in this decision. The architect can give advice on the size and shape most desirable for a church site. He should be able to provide helpful counsel on the relative cost of construction on one site as opposed to another, on the location of utility connections and easements, the meaning and application of zoning and building-code regulations, and sometimes the value of the property under consideration.

The architect can stimulate discussion on key issues without shaping the debate to meet his own preconceptions. He can recommend reading materials, suggest nearby churches for study tours, and encourage committee members to attend conferences and meetings at which they can be exposed to contemporary ecclesiastical art and architecture.

Respective Roles of Architect and Committee

It is the task of both architect and committee to provoke and stimulate the other, with neither blindly accepting the other's opinions or trying to dictate conclusions. This is the ideal, but this ideal is often not realized. Many church buildings are designed by architects who have little idea of the program to be served by the buildings, and, as a result, there are many outdated monuments that are no more than a tribute to the architect's whimsy and caprice.

The first meeting of a building committee that has no clear understanding of its responsibility is apt to be a hodgepodge of assorted prejudices, mistaken zeal, and arbitrary firmness. It is called by a chairman who probably has never served on a similar committee. After a prayer and a long silence, someone announces that in his judgment the first question to decide is whether the church will accept one of "those modern things." A sympathetic colleague immediately casts his vote for a Georgian Colonial building or a "modern Gothic" if the architect insists on a "contemporary" style. Inevitably, a plea is made for a church that "looks like a church" by a member who visualizes the lovely white clapboard meetinghouse he attended as a boy. Nostalgia for the chapel he attended at seminary influences the pastor to suggest that a copy of this lovely monument be erected. The new A-frame mission church building under construction on the edge of town excites a favorable comment or two, especially in view of its low cost per square foot. The "music problem" emerges as an early point of dissension, but most agree that exposed choirs are very nice, although exposed organ pipes are somewhat out of style. The group's aesthete announces that split chancels are the answer to the "chancel problem," provided, of course, a large marble altar with tall imposing candles is placed against the back wall to assure a "worshipful atmosphere." The result: another monstrosity in the making.

At this point the architect may enter the picture. He is not given a thoughtfully developed program but asked to enshrine the varied prejudices of a committee in one building. A patient and skillful architect may salvage something by asking penetrating questions that will graphically demonstrate how much more discussion is required. More likely than not, he will resignedly accept the contract as just another commission and give the committee what it asks for. The committee will probably remain oblivious of the opportunity it has missed for creative exploration of the meaning and life of the church. Architecture, too, is the loser because no architect can do his creative best for a client who has become fixed on a scheme that requires only a draftsman's skills to complete.

The architect and building committee need not issue blank endorsements to each other. The building should not be built if the architect cannot win acceptance from his client. Neither should the architect blindly follow a building program he knows to be deficient. Each has a primary responsibility that should be discharged in a process involving co-operative and imaginative interaction.

The Architect's Fee Contract

These processes of planning a building are not simple or inexpensive. The architect may even be entitled to extra compensation for some of the services a building program requires. The architect must also be fair with the church. At the outset he should describe exactly what he will do for his fee, and the fee contract he proposes should clearly set forth the amount and conditions of his compensation. The circumstances under which any extra compensation may be due should be carefully delineated.*

Recognizing the architect as a businessman is a simple but often neglected obligation of the client. While the architect's fee may appear large, it must be kept in mind that he has to use a considerable portion of the fee to operate his office and secure other professional services. For example, he must employ experts such as structural and mechanical engineers, as well as consultants in acoustics, interior design, and site planning to provide specialized services.

Since time requirements are critical to the architect and constitute a major factor in negotiating the fee, time must not be wasted frivolously in meaningless meetings, social amenities, unnecessary renderings, or redesign. It is astounding how many drawings become valueless because the client did not properly time its requests for architectural drawings. As an example, for a committee to order working drawings before the available funds are clearly determined and the congregation has approved the preliminary design is to court disaster.

Any requests by the client that uselessly involve the architect in detailed drawings deprive the church of valuable time that could be devoted to working with the congregation in planning as well as in design conception. If the dilatory conduct of the church places the architect in a financially untenable position, he may be tempted to push the building to completion with the least possible expenditure of time. It is in the client's interests that the architect's time be devoted to creative architecture, not to compensating for the church's mistakes or doing its busywork.

* See Appendix III for detailed suggestions on selecting an architect and negotiating the contract for services.

--⊰{ ❊ }⊱--

CHAPTER SIX

The Written Program

"Every crucial element in essential planning pivots upon the building
committee's vision of its task and upon its competence. . . . In every
church building program failure that I remember the one constant
factor has been the building committee's failure to see its proper role." [1]
—*The Reverend Edward S. Frey*

Program, architect, and building committee are all essential for good
architecture. Writing the building program is the task of the building committee, which must discharge its responsibilities in such a way
that the talents, insights, and energies of the people within the church
eventually find expression in the creation of the new building.

The word "program" often confuses both congregations and architects. It can, of course, refer to such church activities as rummage sales,
pizza parties, and evening lectures, but here we mean nothing less than
a statement of the very *raison d'être* of the church, including its theology, its purposes, its mission.

A written program is needed even in those situations in which the
new construction will be an addition to an existing building. The
church should carefully review its master plan and weigh the effect of
the proposed buildings on future development. Needs to be met in the
new addition must be described. While the breadth of concern may be
limited if the building needs are not extensive, a study in depth to
survey the present, predict the future, and define what the church proposes to do with the new facility is still required.

Planning to Remodel

If a church plans to remodel, the need for a carefully developed building program becomes even more urgent. Most churches that remodel have first struggled with a prior question: Should the church remain where it is or plan to relocate? A quick decision is usually based on quite superficial information.

In addition, a church which plans to remodel must ask the same kind of basic questions that confront all building committees. Why is remodeling needed? What does the church propose to do with the remodeled building? What are the compelling beliefs and needs of the congregation that require this step? What of the future, its needs and problems?

Remodeling does not mean just knocking out a few partitions and spreading new paint on the walls. It is a serious step that merits the full attention of the church in a concentrated period of study and examination.

Organization of Building Committees

Building programs may be developed in a number of ways. Some are almost wholly prepared or dictated by the clergy; others grow out of a broad involvement of the congregation. Inevitably, the church's polity or system of government will be influential in this process. The recommendations of denominational church building offices and mission boards should be considered and followed whenever feasible.[2] In those churches characterized by a strong hierarchical polity, authorities should take special pains to encourage a broad participation of the parishioners in preparing the program, since buildings imposed by ecclesiastical fiat can easily arouse suspicion and resistance on the part of parishioners.

This phenomenon is clearly seen in many of the new European church buildings so admired by architectural critics. They were designed by excellent architects working in close collaboration with the clergy, but with little congregational involvement. The result in terms of architecture is often outstanding, but these churches are often poorly attended and sometimes even ignored by their parishioners. Churches designed in this manner may serve as beautiful monuments yet remain clergy-centered rather than people-centered.

Nevertheless, there are some valid arguments to be advanced for permitting the entire building program to be prepared by the minister and the architect. It is undoubtedly the least complicated way to go about the task, especially from the architect's point of view. The minister is probably the person who knows the church most intimately and is best informed on current theological thought. He is usually more capable of communicating needs and concepts than most of his congregation. Indeed, unless a congregation is willing to undertake a carefully organized and disciplined study of the related problems, it is probably wiser to leave the planning function to the clergyman and the architect.

Solutions that attempt to strike a middle ground between broad congregational involvement and a clergy-centered approach often prove unsatisfactory. To turn the task over to the "power structure," or controlling board of the church, is apt to result in a building in which utilitarianism prevails over all other considerations. Representatives of a controlling board should, of course, be involved in the planning process but should participate as part of a broader group brought into the decision-making process.

Some churches have had satisfactory results by organizing a building committee composed of representatives of all church organizations. Although such a committee may accurately reflect the concerns of the membership, there is a danger that committees chosen in this way may represent the special interests of official boards or particular groups rather than the whole church. People should be asked to serve on a building committee because of talents, insights, knowledge, inquisitiveness, and ability to learn rather than their political relationships to church structure.

When all arguments are weighed, most churches conclude that the hardest way is still the best—that is, organizing several committees in which a large number of people are given tasks matched to their basic interests and abilities.

Appendix I sets forth, in detail, recommendations for organizing building committees along these lines. The principles are simple. Everyone in the church is given an opportunity to be involved at some point. Some will not act, and some will not act effectively, but the church will not be guilty of failing to ask willing and capable people to serve. The burden should always remain on the member to decline to serve if he is not interested or does not have the time.

Large churches may resist inviting all their members to serve in a study process, although it might be more important for the future well-being of such a church than for a smaller one whose members already know each other well. Being a member of a large congregation can too easily degenerate into attending worship services occasionally, and periodically writing a modest check. Service on a building committee can result in significant involvement for those who otherwise would remain on the side lines.

Committees should be appointed or elected according to the tradition of the church. If the congregation normally elects most of the standing committees, then the congregation should elect the building committee; in other churches, the committees may be appointed by the president or by the governing board of the church. Polity and practice should be respected. The important thing is that the congregation must know what is being done, and must approve the procedure either through its support of the governing boards or by actual vote ratifying the nominations.

Once committees are elected, they must be given tools with which to work. This is where many churches can easily fail by not providing adequate resources. The Bibliography on pages 164–169 sets forth some available materials. Most denominations provide lists of suggested reading materials, as does the office of Church Planning and Architecture, National Council of Churches of Christ.[3] One copy of a book or a pamphlet is not enough; several copies should be available so that more than one person can use the material at the same time.

While the extent of reading required will vary between committees, each person should do some reading, and all must be willing to learn. Few committee members will have had experiences that qualify them as experts, and, even for the few persons with experience, additional reading is desirable. The committeeman who will not read is, however, a less troublesome man than the one who reads a little and then offers superficial conclusions based on his "research."

Content of a Building Program

The immediate goal of the building committee is a written report setting forth its conclusions. Oral agreements are not adequate, as people often interpret spoken words in different ways. The written statement need not be long or pretentious; a simple, precise, and clear summary is all that is required.

If the committees have done their tasks well, the report will constitute a fascinating statement that will also be a means of educating the congregation on all aspects of the church's program. Involving the congregation in the development of the building program should allay suspicions and perhaps build enthusiasm among the constituents; it may also assure support when funds are solicited and the congregation is asked to authorize a mortgage to finance construction.

The written program will contain considerable factual and historical information, including a description of the community, a definition of the parish, an analysis of the activities sponsored by the church-worship and church-school requirements, as well as some projections for the future.

But if this is all the written program contains, it becomes simply a compilation of wants and desires, a calendar of activities and events interspersed with statistics.

If a building is to symbolize architecturally the belief of the church, no congregation should build without coming face to face with its own belief. Thus, the agenda should include the preparation of a statement that encompasses and describes the faith of the church. Without this, the architect will be left to guess what is wanted, or design a church according to his own beliefs.

From belief the church must move to consider what it must do to be faithful to its convictions. The report should analyze with cold objectivity what the congregation has been doing and describe what must be done for it better to fill its role as part of a servant church.

If the counsel of previous chapters has been followed, the architect will have shared in many of the meetings concerned with writing the building program. He will have challenged those decisions that are beyond the province of the committees, and hopefully learned more of what makes the church what it is. The architect should always be free to respond to and criticize the building program, and his suggestions should be given serious consideration.

Some churches argue that such conversation with the architect is a waste of money; he need read only what is written in the program. But the value of genuine understanding cannot be overestimated, and without sustained discussion it is doubtful whether the architect will truly get to know the church. For his part, the architect should not concur with the program if he believes parts of it to be superficial, in error, or ambiguous. Only by criticizing the program and working with the church to resolve any differences can ideas be tested, co-operation fostered, and concepts developed that will find expression in a building that reflects belief and an awareness of Christian mission.

—◦❈◦—

CHAPTER SEVEN

Selecting the Site

"I think it is highly important that we must say two things at one
and the same time: no place is holy, but the presentation of the holy
never occurs without the place. It is not space, but without space and
place, where do we meet it?" [1]
—*Dr. Joseph M. Sittler*

U ntil recent years, church sites were judged in accordance with more
or less standard criteria. They should be large, and the larger
the better; even ten acres was not considered too much if the church
could afford it. A corner site with good visibility was preferred. Height
was desirable, particulary if this made it easier for the architect to
design a "dramatic building," but too much height could make the
site impractical because of development costs.

As broad statements these criteria are still valid. Unfortunately, however, too many churches have concluded they cannot proceed unless
the site meets all of these requirements. This too-strict adherence to
specifications becomes especially critical when relocation is being
thought of, as one of the considerations in every relocation study is
whether or not the present site is adequate. Few church sites acquired
before World War II measure up to accepted standards of acreage,
visibility, and accessibility. If these are viewed as minimum requirements, a decision to relocate is, therefore, almost automatic, especially
with all the additional pressures tempting a church to seek solutions

for its problems by locating in greener fields. A strict judgment that a site is "inadequate" is irresponsible when no consideration is given to program and responsibility to the community in which the church site is located.

In the case of new churches, the decision in regard to a site has usually already been made. If the property has been purchased by the denomination before the congregation is gathered, the church should nevertheless evaluate it carefully; denominational executives have been known to make serious mistakes as a result of inadequate knowledge of the history and political makeup of a given area. Laymen in the church can sometimes discover a better site because they have a more intimate understanding of the community and its people. No newly organized church should erect its first unit until it has confirmed that its site is the best available for the work it wishes to do.

In other words, no one can promulgate minimum standards for sites that will fit all situations. Many churches have carried on programs of great significance without large acreage. In a given situation, an established location may be more important than visibility. Visibility and accessibility are guidelines as to what a site should be, but the ultimate question is: *How suited is it as a place for the church to carry out its Christian mission?*

Co-operative Church Planning

Another important question is whether the site fulfills the requirements of co-operative church planning in the community. One of the sadder examples of the failure of churches to plan co-operatively is the windward side of Oahu, Hawaii. There the landowner assigned a strip of land some two blocks long to church uses and offered sites to any church that would agree to build a building. As of 1965, seven churches have erected buildings representing as many denominations. At a time when the ecumenical movement is having a profound impact throughout Christendom, there is nothing so disillusioning and reminiscent of ruthless denominational competition as to drive by "church row" and read the shopping-center-type signs inviting the customer to pick his brand of Christianity.

Co-operative church planning is often referred to as "comity," an arrangement that had its beginning in New England in some proposals made by the Reverend Washington Gladden, a New England Congregationalist, in a series of articles published in *The Century Magazine* in 1882. Gladden argued that Protestantism is best served by fewer churches of a medium to large size rather than by a large number of small churches, and that denominational names were relatively unimportant to most persons seeking church membership. These general principles gained wide acceptance throughout the Northeastern and North Central States, but found little acceptance in the South, thereby setting a pattern that can still be seen today. Many denominations participated in comity agreements, including the Presbyterians, Congregationalists, Evangelical and Reformed, Methodists, Disciples of Christ, and others, but its results are quite imperfect, with its idealistic aims sometimes compromised by denominational competition.[2]

There are several reasons why comity has not fulfilled its early promise, perhaps the most important being the failure of denominations to accept the comity committee as a place for creative planning rather than a means of preventing competition. The committee has often simply been a policeman, with powers to veto proposals, rather than a creative innovator and planner.

One example of this failure is the so-called "one-mile rule," which is still applied with varying degrees of success in many sections of the country. As usually interpreted, this rule prohibited a church belonging to a denomination that had joined in the comity agreement from locating within one mile of any other comity church. While this rule has value in some communities, it ignores the fact that not every parish can be defined as a geographic area with a radius of one mile, and that people do not always attend the church nearest them. In some cases, too, it may be more important to have several churches located in the centers of community activity than to decide arbitrarily that a one-mile radius must separate them.

Where the rule was followed, there were several obvious results. The "noncooperative" denominations were free, of course, to violate its requirements, and in many cases these churches simply took over sites that the "comity" churches would have otherwise developed. Laymen had understandable difficulty in understanding why comity, instituted as a venture in cooperation, was sometimes permitted to heighten denominational competition for "high potential" areas. Of even more serious consequence, at a time when planners were attempting to recover a semblance of unity in community life, the one-mile rule acted to diffuse churches throughout the community, emphasizing its separate elements rather than those held in common.

In other areas comity agreements have been superseded by a new approach: instead of providing policing services in the hope that competition will be curtailed, church planning is seen as a process that looks at the religious needs of an area and seeks to provide answers for those needs. There are no hard and fast rules; churches are urged to locate in specific areas because they are needed there, not because some denomination has filed an early claim for a "comity" allocation.

At its best, such planning is done on a regional, not a community, basis. In this way a comprehensive strategy is developed, making it possible not only to employ professional staff who are trained in planning, but to use regionally developed data, which is often much more complete and reliable. In addition, regional planning is practical because denominational officials, whose support and cooperation are vital, usually work on a regional basis.

Planning should also be wedded to research. Intelligent decision-making is impossible unless it is based on correct information. In fact, one of the reasons comity so often failed was that comity committees seldom had the information they needed for intelligent decisions. Since research is expensive, one of the factors encouraging denominations to work together is the possibility that in this manner they might obtain data which they could not otherwise afford. Churches and denominations can be expected increasingly to form regional research and planning offices with responsibilities for recommending appropriate locations for church sites.

Even if there is neither church planning nor comity in a community, there is no excuse for a church to act irresponsibly. With diligence, study, and survey work, it can develop its own statement of church-planning standards and apply them in selecting a site. Nor should the existence of limited comity be taken as a reason for failure to follow good church-planning principles.

In addition to the help that can be obtained through comity procedures and church-planning offices, each church will require additional information on which to base its final decisions. This is the primary task of the Survey Committee (see Appendix I). This committee should develop a comprehensive body of information about the community in which the church plans to locate—its people and its needs—all of which will be a part of the written building program.

Effects of Urbanization

Since World War II most new and relocating churches have sought sites in residential communities. In some respects this was an outgrowth of "comity" rules that spread churches throughout the community. The movement of many traditional church supporters to the suburbs, the availability of land, and the opportunity for quick growth were other factors in this process. The movement has become so strong that many churches now assume that the only sites worth considering are those situated in the midst of new homes. This has resulted in ecclesiastical blinders which have prevented the churches from recognizing the results of urbanization. However, people often select churches that are some distance from their homes. They may be motivated by theological reasons, a denominational preference, admiration for a particular minister, or sympathy for the kind of program the church sponsors. And with urbanization, people have been dispersed across a broad spectrum of society and culture. Thus a residentially based church finds it more and more difficult to minister to all the needs of people. The church which today wishes to become once again a conscience for the community will have difficulty filling this office if it is built on a narrow residential base and does not represent the whole community. (For a discussion of this concept, see pages 17–18.)

This does not mean that residential parishes should be abandoned; the problem arises when most churches assume this is the only need to be met. In selecting a new site the congregation should adopt the broadest possible vision of its responsibilities—and act accordingly!

Size and Shape Requirements

If land is available, a site of generous proportion is desirable. Generally, a site breaks down into approximately one-third for parking; one-third for landscaping, walkways, and setback requirements; and one-third for buildings.

Most churches feel that three acres is the minimum needed in an average suburban situation, while others believe that five, six, and up to ten or more acres are needed. As a general rule, it is better to acquire too much than too little; the unneeded land can usually be sold, but adjoining parcels can seldom be acquired later except at an exorbitant price. On the other hand, the cost of landscaping and maintaining a large site is substantial, and this can divert large sums that might better be used to finance the program.

The best estimate is up to five acres for a congregation of not more than 700 to 1,000 members. Again, this is no absolute; not all churches need to have five acres, or four, or even one acre. The size of the site must always be related to program, cost, land availability, and location.

Shape can also be important. Most zoning laws and some deed restrictions dictate that buildings cannot be erected within a specified distance of the boundary line. These can make long, narrow, or irregularly shaped sites difficult to develop, since the setback requirements apply to all the boundaries of the property and thus further limit the full utilization of the site. A site that is square, or almost so, is usually the best one for maximum use of land.

Zoning and Deed Restrictions

Zoning regulations limit the use of land and sometimes specify that churches cannot be erected in residential zones. Similarly, some deeds have restrictions specifically excluding church use. These restrictions present problems that must be solved before the site is acquired.

If zoning regulations prevent church use of property, there is always the possibility that a special-use permit can be obtained. Sometimes it requires legal counsel, as well as a great deal of tact, to convince nearby property owners that the church will not be a nuisance in the community. A contract to purchase property that has not received zoning clearance should carry a provision that the purchase may be rescinded and the earnest money returned if required zoning permits cannot be obtained or special-use permits authorized.

Deed restrictions can be a more vexing problem. While zoning regulations are subject to change by planning and zoning boards, deed restrictions cannot be changed without following prescribed procedures, which can be complicated and expensive. One type restricts the height of buildings; others provide additional setback requirements, limit the kind of buildings that can be erected, or specify that residences only may be built on the property. Failure to abide by deed restrictions may subject the church to various penalties, such as court decrees enjoining it from using the property, or even forfeiture of title to the party who imposed the restriction.

While it is obviously foolish for a church to accept title to property on which a church cannot be built, it is almost equally shortsighted to accept title to property that can be used only by a church. This is true even if the property comes as a gift, since the restriction serves to fix the church in one location; it cannot move and salvage its investment unless it can find some other church willing to buy the property—and few will be interested in paying a substantial sum for a clouded title. Banks may even refuse to lend money to a church with a title so restricted, as the market for the building would be very limited in the event of foreclosure.

Developers of large housing projects are the source of another kind of restriction that can cause trouble. Recognizing that churches attract buyers for residential properties, a real-estate developer may sell land to a congregation only if it agrees to build within a specified period of time—usually a very short time. Accepting such a requirement can force a church into a costly and premature building program—that is, building before there are sufficient people in the new community to support the program. If such an agreement is suggested, the church should bargain for a clause exempting it from performance if the population does not reach a specified level by the deadline set for the beginning of construction.

Deed restrictions may be found in a declaration of restrictions filed at the time the plat was recorded, or in the deed of the property to the church, or they may be in a deed of the property to a prior owner. Since the possibility and effect of restrictions cannot be ignored, a careful title search is always imperative. If restrictions exist, it is incumbent on the church to understand their provisions and be prepared to abide by their terms, or not buy the property.

Other Special Factors Affecting Site Feasibility

Highway departments should be consulted for information on projections for widening roads, building new roads, or constructing limited-access highways. Since road widening is almost always inevitable in a growing community, a site should be deep enough so that any reasonable road widening would not destroy its usefulness.

Traffic patterns constitute valuable information; a church needs to be on a traveled road, but not on a site whose accessibility is impaired by unusually heavy traffic. Public transportation is no longer as important a factor as it once was, although it may have considerable importance in some areas.

Such geographical barriers as major highways, railroads, and publicly owned lands should be studied carefully, since they tend to cut off and insulate areas, often creating psychological barriers which are difficult to overcome. A church site should not be located with its back against a barrier that might limit its outreach to three sides.

It would be wise to consult land-use maps prepared by developers or zoning agencies for information on parks, cemeteries, and other services that will take large blocks of land out of use. Any church will have difficulty if it is in the middle of a large area of land set aside for such purposes.

The location of land acquired by the school board for future school expansion is another important factor. Projections of school growth should be analyzed and compared with those of other communities. Church sites near newly erected schools are frequently well located, as many of the same factors that influence school officials in the selection of sites are also important to a church.

Corner properties often make good sites, but it is well to check the owner's responsibility for street, sewer, curb, and sidewalk construction. Since setback requirements apply to both streets, this factor can seriously limit the amount of land on a corner site that can be devoted to buildings.

Visibility is obviously a considerable asset, since people seeing the church are reminded that it exists. Visibility is also a help in finding the church and is to be considered when weighing the accessibility of a particular site. A striking location on a high elevation may lend itself to creative architectural expression, but dramatic sites usually require extensive and expensive improvements.

Soil tests are often desirable to determine whether there will be a problem in building on the property. If the site is not level, it is important to evaluate elevations in reference to roads and drainage. Adjoining properties should be studied to see if there is any danger of substantial drainage from them onto the site. A check list of other relevant questions would include the following: Will the site require unusual expenditures for landscaping? Where are the utility connections located? Are winds apt to be a problem if the church decides to erect a tower or steeple? Where are the easements for gas, electricity, telephones, and sewers located, and will their location affect the use of the site? What are the taxes on the property? Is the church entitled to exemption for taxes, and, if so, what must be done to claim that exemption? Are there any special assessments, or will there be *future* assessments for streets, sewers, sidewalks, or curbs? Does the seller possess a recent survey? Should the church require a new survey to be made? *

The Architect's Role in Site Selection

Needless to say, in helping the church evaluate the factors involved in choosing a site, the architect can be very helpful. He can analyze the construction problems relating to a particular property; he can point out graphically how zoning, parking, setback, and other requirements will affect the design of the building. He will be able to offer counsel on soil tests and site-development costs. In most cases, the architect is not only willing but anxious to have an opportunity to work with the church when the critical decision on a site is being made.

If a possible site measures up in most—but not all—respects, the most creative minds in the church should investigate ways to compensate for the deficiencies of the site. If it is not large enough to provide adequate parking, other parking facilities may be found at nearby schools, public buildings, shopping centers, even filling stations. If the site is uneconomical because of its cost (and this is often the case where land is acquired in the downtown sections of cities), the church should analyze the possibility of vertical construction on a smaller plot, with a portion of the building leased to other nonprofit groups, or perhaps even businesses. No possibilities should be left unexplored, once it is clear that a particular piece of property is the best location from which a given church can carry out its responsibilities.

* See Appendix II for a list of other pertinent questions to be asked concerning property to be used as a church site.

---*❧ ❋ ☙*---

CHAPTER EIGHT

The Master Plan

"Absolute certainty we cannot have. We don't know the future and perhaps never will. But we should not fear to predict the predictable because we are unable to predict the unpredictable." [1]
—*Constantinos Doxiadis*

This eminently practical advice by one of the world's great planners is most appropriate for a church building committee. Most churches find it impossible to build all the needed facilities at one time. Often there are financial limitations which restrict the ability to build. In other cases a portion of the building must be postponed until anticipated growth in membership and program occurs. Some churches may not be able to anticipate future growth but nevertheless want to reserve some land in the event increased program needs require additional buildings. In all of these cases, while there are unknown elements which make it difficult to predict accurately the extent of future requirements, churches are not relieved of the obligation to develop as careful a master plan as is possible under the circumstances.

Even a casual examination of church buildings will disclose that many congregations have not taken master planning seriously. This is often seen in the clashing of styles between two units designed according to different architectural concepts. Poorly placed parking lots; awkward circulation patterns; long, twisting passageways and stair wells; windowless spaces or spaces with too much light—all these are telltale signs. Dozens of little-used chapel churches can be seen that were once first units, but now sit awkwardly and discordantly where one would normally expect to see the principal worship building. Occasionally, the result is so unsatisfactory that relocation or remodeling becomes imperative. Wasted spaces, clashing aesthetics, questionable tastes are often the result of an architect and a church failing to take the time to appraise intelligently future building requirements.

On the other hand, it is possible to overplan. Churches and architects can be carried away with their dreams of the future, even to the extent of preparing detailed working drawings for buildings they hope will be needed someday. This is foolish. No church should proceed from a first unit to a second unit without a careful reconsideration of all the basic assumptions that were the basis for the master plan. New circumstances may suggest necessary or advisable changes. Perhaps the membership growth once projected has not occurred, or, again, it may have exceeded expectations. Perhaps there have been major changes in the Christian education program, or a whole new field of mission responsibility requiring different facilities may have presented itself since the first buildings were erected. Experience may have shown that some elements of the original plan were the result of congregational immaturity and should now be revised. While a church should not casually abandon a master plan, it should always be open to re-examination. Unfortunately, if the church has expended a large sum for an overly detailed master plan, it may be loath to authorize changes, regardless of their necessity.

Basic Requirements for a Master Plan

The master plan should illustrate the location and interrelationship of the principal building elements proposed for the church site. Unless the whole complex is to be built at one time, detailed working drawings are not needed; they might simply be schematic drawings, so called because they show the scheme, or plan, for the principal parts but not the detail of the proposed construction. The reason for this, of course, is that detailed working drawings require a great deal of time to prepare and are, consequently, expensive.

If not all the buildings are to be erected at once, a master plan should show how the first buildings will be used in the future, as well as the planned use for buildings to be put up later. The interrelationship between sections of buildings erected at different times requires careful study, since the uses to which the first buildings are assigned often change when the second section of buildings is erected. It is important, therefore, that the master plan show how the buildings will be used, not only in the ultimate scheme, but also at the various stages of construction.

A master plan should also assure a continuity and coherence of style, but part of its function is to provide for the unexpected. Church surveys can seriously underestimate future needs. If space is available, the master plan should preserve some options for the future so that the church can adapt its buildings easily and economically to changing program requirements.

Traffic Problems and Their Effect

One of the tasks of the architect is to solve the mundane problem of traffic control. Automobiles are part, but not all, of the problem; the architect also has to consider where people are likely to walk. Failure to consider walking habits can result in impressive front doors which are largely unused because most persons find a side or back door more convenient.

In most communities, regulations specify the number of parking places the church is to provide. The problem of providing adequate parking is more complicated, however, than simply designating a certain area or a master plan that satisfies zoning regulations; this is because the parking area must be carefully co-ordinated with the flow of traffic on adjoining streets. The directions in which cars will travel as they enter the site, the places where passengers can be discharged, the effect of snow and ice on traffic flow, the point of exit for the cars, whether any of the adjoining streets are limited to one-way traffic—all these factors have to be taken into consideration.

In studying a proposed master plan, the committee should try to visualize how traffic patterns will work out in practice. Each person should mentally trace the way he will travel to the church site, that is, will he be able to turn into the site from the street? Does the plan provide for one way to enter and another way to leave? (Two-way traffic into a parking area may be asking for trouble.) Will it be possible to discharge passengers at a protected spot, particularly in bad weather, without halting the flow of traffic? Will it be possible for someone who is disabled to leave a car and travel up or down a ramp and thus enter the church building? Does the architect's proposal provide for the maximum use of the parking area without putting cars too close together? (Space must also be reserved for cars to back out of parking places.) Will it be possible to erect signs that clearly instruct people on the traffic pattern to be followed? Are the building entrances co-ordinated with the parking area and the paths people are likely to follow from the parking area?

There is no unanimity of opinion as to where the parking area should be placed—in front or in back, in a hidden or obvious place. A reasonable rule of thumb is to make the parking lot obvious enough so that people who are looking for it will not be confused, but secluded enough so that the church buildings do not appear to be ships adrift in a sea of blacktop.

Other Factors: Location of Parsonage, Landscape Requirements, Need for a Basement

Differences of opinion are also evident in regard to the location of the parsonage. Many argue that it should be placed near the church—adjoining the church site, if possible; others believe it should be some distance away. If a church decides that the parsonage should adjoin the church property, it becomes a factor to be considered in developing the master plan. The architect and building committee will want to consider not only such things as land use but also the plan of vehicular traffic and the need of the minister's family for privacy.

Some church buildings seem to be built with little or no regard to landscape planning, apparently relying on parish organizations to supply plantings on a somewhat hit-or-miss basis. This kind of carelessness is inexcusable. A landscape architect can be employed to draw up a master landscape plan to be implemented as funds become available. If a church cannot afford to landscape its entire site at one time, the master plan is a simple way to make sure that the right shrubs, trees, and flowers are so planted as ultimately to achieve a harmonious result. Since such a plan is only a small percentage of the building budget, a church would be wise to ask its architect to develop an over-all plan in collaboration with a competent landscape architect.

Whether a church should build a basement depends in great measure on the size and configuration of the property. If a church selects its site in terms of the best place to carry out mission responsibility, it may well be necessary to build "vertically"—that is, erect a building of more than one story. In such a case, a basement is a logical solution. The configuration of some sites may also make a basement advisable. Since building on the side of a steep incline is always more expensive than on level ground, the addition of a basement may capture additional rooms with "daylight" windows at little extra cost.

The same saving is not always possible for church buildings erected on relatively level sites. Basement rooms in buildings on level sites are not of the same quality as rooms on the ground floor, and the cost of these rooms can often be as much as if the same amount of floor space had been provided in a separate or larger building with all rooms at ground level.

Building a basement usually results in rooms that have very little natural light, are awkwardly arranged, and are built at no real saving. If the site is large enough and does not have unusual characteristics, most building experts agree that a church receives much more adequate building space without an appreciable increase in costs if all of its facilities are of single-story construction.

Correcting Past Mistakes

For many congregations, the problem of master planning is how to correct the mistakes previous generations have made. The first unit may have been a chapel located on the precise spot that should have been reserved for the principal worship building. Or it may have been a chapel building too large to serve as a chapel and too small to be adequate as a permanent worship center. The design of the "inherited" buildings is frequently unsatisfactory, and it is obvious that the original concept of the first buildings should not be continued.

In these circumstances a few churches sell their property and begin anew. Occasionally this can be done without serious financial loss. Others, either for financial reasons or because they have become established in a particular place, feel that such a move is impossible. Perhaps a new site cannot be obtained, or the church simply does not have the money to tear down its inadequate structure and build a new one. These churches—and their architects—must find some way for the errors of the past to be minimized and camouflaged. Although much harm has already been done, a master plan will at least assure the church that the proposed new building will not make the situation worse, and will also help in evaluating a new design solution proposed by the architect.

Architect's Fees for Master Planning

The American Institute of Architects recommends that all contracts for the design of a church building include a clause to describe the kind of extra services the architect must render if he is to prepare the master plan.* Before a contract is signed, the architect and the church should discuss quite frankly the method and amount of compensation for services to be rendered in the preparation of a master plan. It is not unusual for an architect to charge an additional sum; sometimes this is a flat fee, sometimes an additional percentage related to the estimated construction costs for all the work projected by the master plan. The church should not expect the architect to provide a master plan as part of the agreed percentage of the cost of the first buildings to be erected unless this is specifically agreed to at the time the fee contract is signed.

Selecting a "First Unit"

Churches that decide they cannot erect all their buildings at one time face the task of deciding which part to build first. The first unit is often a compromise between what is realistically possible and what the church would do if finances and program permitted. Solving this problem can be one of the most difficult decisions a congregation has to make.

A few general principles should be observed. Every church should provide an adequate place for corporate worship, although this need not be a long-term solution. Some kind of a decision is needed to

* See Appendix III, pp. 148–153.

carry out educational and fellowship programs within the limits of the first building unit. Such a decision does not require that space be provided for all the church's proposed activities, but advance planning should establish priorities and determine what will have to be eliminated or housed elsewhere until additional facilities can be built.

There is no ideal choice for a "first unit." Many would elect to build the permanent worship building, often called the sanctuary, but there are serious problems to be overcome if this decision is to be carried out successfully. One should recognize that the worship unit is the most expensive to build, often calling for expensive furnishings, and sometimes carpeting and an organ. In addition, such a building is not subject to easy multiple use.

Building the permanent worship unit first presents special difficulties for new or relocating churches that anticipate substantial future growth, since the seating capacity is usually frozen when the worship unit is built. If designed for the present membership, the danger is that the building will be obsolete within a few years. If designed with adequate seating for future growth, the unused seating can present a psychological problem, while requiring a substantial financial investment with no prospect of early returns either in program or people. Some architects have attempted to solve this by ingenious plans that will permit easy remodeling and expansion at a future date, but most of these solutions leave something to be desired.

If the permanent worship building is erected first, the church faces the serious problem of where to house the church school and other activities. Since the worship building is usually not suitable for these activities, the only solution may be to rent facilities elsewhere or use parishioners' homes—with all the resulting problems.

Some churches have attempted to solve the problem by building a chapel as the first unit. This is sometimes the most satisfactory solution as it provides the church with a good place for worship that is not so large as to be a poor stewardship of resources, and yet can serve as a symbol of congregational unity and Christian witness. The problems of Christian education and service activities must still be solved, but a chapel usually costs less than a worship unit and thus may release funds for a supplementary building.

The principal disadvantage of building the chapel as the first unit is the difficulty of using it for anything other than worship. Also, hopes of effecting economies through this approach are sometimes disappointing, since the square-foot or cubic-foot cost of a chapel is quite high, and if pews and an organ are part of the plan, the amount "saved" will be sharply reduced. Size can also be a problem, as a chapel large enough to serve as a first unit may be too large to be used efficiently after the permanent worship building is erected.

Neither is building education space first a very satisfactory answer. Such an area can often be used in service activities by judiciously omitting a few partitions and installing a kitchenette, but this does not often satisfy the need for a satisfactory worship center. Unable to resolve these objections, many churches have opted for a hall that is used initially for worship but will eventually be a place for fellowship and service activities. This solution often offers the most square footage for the money, and there are fewer objections to using this kind of building for other activities. Since pews are not practical, there is no temptation to freeze the space to one use by installing them, but with sensitive treatment a very satisfactory worship space can be provided. Some people may have difficulty worshiping in a room that is also used for many other purposes, but the situation might also provide the congregation with an occasion for thoughtful reflection on the meaning of sacred space and its relationship to secular activity.

Nevertheless, there are some disadvantages in this approach. If a master plan is properly developed, the hall will often be placed on a less prominent portion of the site, and this may result in an unsatisfactory over-all appearance that cannot be corrected until the worship building is erected. Various paraphernalia and furnishings may provide a clever camouflage, but to many people halls will remain halls, and thus poorly suited for worship. Sometimes size becomes a problem: for example, a fellowship hall that fits very nicely in a master plan may seem too large when used by a relatively small congregation for worship.

There really is no "right answer." Since the needs of each church vary, a congregation faced with the question must carefully weigh all the facts and reach the decision that appears to best satisfy its particular goals.

--⊰ ✳ ⊱--

PART THREE

Form, Function, and Belief

Form follows function, but a form that reflects
no more than function is sterile. Form must
also reflect belief—belief in God, belief about
ourselves, belief about the world in which we
live and work. Function, belief, mission—these
are the guides for creating meeting places
for the covenanted people of faith.

---◦◖ ❉ ◗◦---

CHAPTER NINE

Places for Worship

"Architecture has nothing to do with the various 'styles.' The styles
are to architecture what a feather is on a woman's head; it is
something pretty, though not always, and never anything more.
Architecture has graver ends." [1]

—*Le Corbusier*

Most church building committees will do the necessary homework
to investigate finances and plan administrative facilities, but in
its decisions on worship facilities, sentimentality and irrelevant traditions too often prevail over study, research, and careful evaluation.
Think, for example, of the traditionalism that makes most building
committees assume that candles are a necessary part of an altar; similarly, reading desks and lecterns are thought to be required, simply
because no one on the building committee has ever seen a church without them. In some churches, flowers have become such an absolute
requirement that they are allowed to engulf the altar/table, and flags
are constantly placed before congregations either because of sentimentality or a misguided sense of patriotism. Even the use of pews
has taken on such an automatic character that few committees examine
their history or whether they are satisfactory places for people to sit.
A worship committee that accepts such "traditions" without raising
basic questions often becomes the agent by which the past is preserved
without reason, understanding, or concern for the future. Since the

style, tone, and quality of the whole building may be set by the place that is designed for worship, the committee must be more objective, possess greater imagination, and exhibit more courage than any other group involved in a building program.

People assigned to worship committees are often the most loyal members, with a long history of deep involvement in the life of the church. This very fact, however, may create problems, since their many years of service may lead many to assume that their opinions on worship are almost sacrosanct in character. They are apt to skip basic questions and jump immediately to final decisions on where the choir should be placed, whether the church should have a lectern, and where the altar or table should be located.

Worship committees should begin with one basic question: What is contemporary Christian worship? An understanding of history will offer many insights, and can also help to free us from any tendency to traditionalism for its own sake. A custom should be retained only if a study of its origin, coupled with an appreciation of the added meaning contributed by history, convinces the committee of its value for contemporary worship. Other customs, which may be based on arbitrary reasons or a theology to which the congregation could no longer give assent, may be quietly discarded.

The committee cannot avoid the most fundamental questions: What is preaching today, and what place should it have in the worship life of the congregation? Why do we have a choir and what is its role in services? Why has the church often used an altar, or table, as one of its foci for worship, and what meaning should its use have today? What is the significance of baptism in the life of the congregation? What is the place of the Bible in contemporary worship?

Importance and Role of Christian Worship

The story of worship in the Christian church reveals a variety of practices and traditions. Some issues, however, will be encountered by any church engaged in building a place for worship: for example, the importance of corporate public worship, the role of private meditation, the location of appropriate foci for worship.

Professor James F. White has analyzed Christian worship from a historical viewpoint and has concluded that there are essentially two approaches. "Privatized" worship places a special emphasis on individual feelings; a person simply receives the emotional stimuli that put him in a "worshipful mood." A worship experience of this type can be the result of fiery oratory, an inspiring choir, skillful lighting, or awe-inspiring architecture.[2]

Another kind of worship consists of an active response by a corporate body—a group of people bound together by a common belief. This is the work of people who come together to confess their sins and respond to God's mercy through common praise, thanksgiving, and the sacraments. The emphasis is on the fact that the faithful constitute a community that belongs to God. Private devotions are important, but worship must involve the whole church in a common public act.

This awareness is at the heart of what is popularly called the "liturgical movement," the primary aim of which is to draw the people of the congregation into active participation in the act of worship. To some, the word "liturgy" is associated only with those churches with elaborate and repetitive rituals, but, literally, liturgy means the work of people in worship of God, and, in this sense, all churches have a liturgy.

The liturgical movement has had a profound effect on the church buildings of Europe, both Catholic and Protestant. This is seen in their style, spatial qualities, and arrangements, which coupled with the development of new materials and construction techniques, have brought forth in the decades since 1920 the best churches in centuries—buildings designed by such architects as Rudolph Schwarz, Karl Moser, August Perret, Dominikus Bohn, Fritz Metzger, Herman Baur, and others.

The excellence of these buildings lies in the fact that they not only imaginatively utilize contemporary construction methods, but that their design is theologically informed and sensitive to the importance of congregational involvement in public worship. At a time when most new American churches were being designed to accommodate a performing clergy and choir, these European pioneers were experimenting with ways in which the church and the people could be brought into a closer relationship.

The Constitution on the Sacred Liturgy, promulgated at Vatican Council II, officially recognized many of the principles that had been rediscovered in the liturgical renewal. A study of the guidebooks published in recent years to aid priests in implementing the Constitution is revealing—and challenging—to a Protestant. The guidebooks make it clear that worship is to be public, that the church is not the priest but the people, that "there are no private sacraments, since Christ has chosen to sanctify men by acting in and through his Church, which is a community." They sharply criticize the priest who acts as Moses, "alone with God on the mountain," while the "people are afar off, mere spectators waiting to receive something." [3]

It is too soon to know whether this will be reflected in American Catholic church buildings which will be erected in coming years. In American Protestantism, however, lack of interest in liturgical renewal until recent years has meant that most of its church buildings imply an understanding of worship as consisting primarily of people sitting as observers while they are sung to, spoken to, and prayed for.

Few people appreciate how a building can frustrate a church in its effort to break down barriers between people. Churches try to make everyone "feel at home," with fellowship dinners, by placing "greeters" at the door, and cautioning members to "be sure to greet the strangers." Such efforts have merit, but these same congregations ought to recognize that the awe-inspiring, personality-crushing buildings in which strangers are invited to worship may contribute to their feeling of anonymity and isolation.

Fortunately, many Protestants are becoming increasingly aware of how far they have departed from their origins. As one critic sharply put it, . . . "it is to the shame of the Reformed that while the Christian brethren who are most tightly bound by tradition are recapturing this biblical teaching of the family of God and expressing it in their architecture, so many of the children of the Reformation are setting up altars appropriate only for a high Roman doctrine of the Mass as the re-sacrifice of Christ." [4] Some Presbyterians can now see how far they have moved from sixteenth-century Calvinists; Congregationalists from the Puritans; Methodists from the Wesleyan movement of the eighteenth century. The concern is not a matter simply of re-establishing primitive traditions; such a re-examination should, however, lead us back to basic inquiries of biblical faith and the nature of the church.

One of the basic truths of the Reformers certainly needs re-emphasis: The congregation is a community representing the "priesthood of believers." In such a community, clearly, there is no separation between priest and laity, although some may be called to perform different functions in accordance with individual talents, skills, and calling.

In many ways this concept of the gathered community contradicts a point of view that sees the church as a militant army of pilgrims, an approach that has had wide currency and is sometimes used to justify long, dark, narrow church buildings. Such buildings can easily destroy identity among worshipers and re-create the privatized worship of the Middle Ages as something that happened to the individual, not an action that a group of people carried out as part of its common faith.

Experiments in Architectural Forms

In recent years there have been a number of experiments in structural forms by churches seeking to catch this spirit of the gathered community. One temporarily popular architectural solution, the circular church, is now seen to have serious functional difficulties. In such a building, it is almost impossible to avoid an overemphasis on the altar, with a correlative diminution of the other points of liturgical interest. Such churches force people to sit in a circle because they are considered a family, forgetting that a family does not sit in a circle unless that is the best way to carry out a common activity.

Others have more successfully incorporated this concept in buildings which permit seating in a semicircle. The congregation is placed in close proximity to one another, as well as to the foci of worship. Functionally the arrangement can work quite satisfactorily while still preserving the intimacy of the gathered group. Frequently, chairs rather than pews are used, thus making it possible to vary the physical arrangements from week to week, depending on the kind of worship service which will take place.

Most significant experiments are occurring in those churches which seek to break down the traditional separation between the sacred and the secular by erecting worship facilities that can be used in a variety of ways and for a number of purposes. Davies, in his important work *The Secular Use of Church Buildings,* argues that the secular use of church buildings is not only appropriate to today's needs but consistent with the attitudes and practices of the early Christian church. To him, an Anglican, worship is not something that happens "between the Church and God, but between the world and God, the Church being no more than an instrument." [5] Thus the multipurpose worship space is seen not as a temporary expedient that is economical and practical, but as the logical outgrowth of contemporary thought.

There are problems, however. Davies also reports a survey that asked persons to express their reactions to a variety of activities taking place in the worship building. Parish meetings, lectures, plays, children's activities, and concerts were approved, but more than half of those queried refused to sanction socials, films, dances, and ballet. Those approving plays and concerts specified an additional limitation; only those plays and concerts were permissible that carried a "religious" theme or were of a classical nature.[6] Thus, while giving assent to some secular activities, the good church people insisted on retaining the traditional dichotomy by casting a sacred mantle over those secular activities they would tolerate.

Nevertheless, many churches are beginning to erect worship facilities which are designed specifically to be multipurpose in character. These churches challenge the basic assumption many of us have held, that churches should serve as sacred retreat centers from the world. The willingness to accept varied activities within the worship space invariably influences the worship practices of the congregation by suggesting a large number of options for worship practices. On occasion, worship can center on the Lord's Supper, on another it can include a film, discussion, music other than the traditional, a play, dialogue, even a "happening" which requires active congregational participation. The possibilities are virtually limitless. Younger persons almost always respond enthusiastically, but those who expect a structured style of worship which is seldom varied are usually disquieted. Persons who are open to new kinds of experiences often find that this varied style of worship provides a much-needed enrichment for their spiritual lives.

Interior Character of Buildings and its Effect on Worship

Architecture must be judged not only by the structural form of the building and its visual impact on the surrounding environment, but also by the kind of space that is created within it. A building can present an outward appearance that satisfies all of the requirements for good church architecture and still be a failure. The relationship between a worshiper and the space in which he worships is so intimate and intense that the wrong spatial qualities can destroy even the possibility of worship. As was suggested in Chapter 5, building committees should always describe the qualities that will best reflect their beliefs and worship needs.

If the spatial relationships are to minimize the separation between people and clergy, the environment should be one in which people will easily and willingly participate in a common act. A spatial language is needed to express the idea of a Christian community called to discipleship. A church wants to remind those present that God is seen both within and outside the world, a paradox architects understandably find difficult to reduce to spatial terms. High vertical thrusts have sometimes been employed to capture the otherworldly character of God. If this is done, however, it is also important that the vertical be balanced by a horizontal thrust, suggesting that God can also be found in the world about us. As a counterpoint to the traditional emphasis on the otherworldliness of the Gospel, structure and the space it creates should suggest the earthiness and directness of the Gospel and its concern for the day-to-day needs of people.

Creating space compatible with Christian worship does not so much mean high ceilings and sweeping roofs as the arrangement of people, the utilization of natural lighting, and the relationship between the congregation and the things that have come to have religious significance: pulpit, table, and font. With modern technology and engineering, a church can produce an appropriate "atmosphere" for every occasion. Underground buildings can have a simulated "natural" environment, temperature can be regulated within a building at all times, and lighting can be used to invoke any mood desired. While such techniques have no doubt served to make many of the places in which we live or work more habitable, something goes wrong when this same contrived approach is applied to a church building. For example, artificial plantings seem to contradict the authenticity of Christian worship. Rheostats installed in elaborate switchboards are effective in a theater, but in the church they can make the worshiper feel he is being tricked into reverence. In "creating the right atmosphere," architects have often failed because they have tried to create artificially what they were incapable of creating naturally.

"Creating an atmosphere for worship" is a phrase often used both by churchmen and by architects. Although the phrase is not objectionable if used within the context of a description of the design process, it should be remembered that a great church building is not the result of a created atmosphere. Rather it is a place created out of an understanding of the worship needs of the congregation, without contrivance or deception. Its spatial qualities should complement and supplement the belief of the worshiping community and make it easy to draw people together in common spirit.

Foci for Worship

E. A. Sövik, formerly President of the Guild for Religious Architecture of the American Institute of Architects, has suggested that it would be much easier to involve the whole congregation in corporate worship if "we will not insist that the church space has to have a single strong focus." He argues that there should be many foci, so that the "congregation can sometimes feel itself to be the center, and sometimes the pulpit, and sometimes the table, and sometimes the choir, a prayer desk, the reading desk, the baptismal font." The focus would move to wherever the action of the liturgy naturally takes it. His plea is that worship should be more than a dialogue between the chancel and the nave, but a "varied action involving voices from a number of other positions." [7]

Although difficult to implement architecturally, Sövik's comments merit serious consideration. It is surely a mistake for a church to center all its worship on one of its aspects. Worship committees have a very important task in determining which foci are appropriate and which are extraneous or unsuitable, especially since church buildings are filled with so many possibilities. For example, most altars or tables have candles placed upon them, and, of course, the cross is a common point of focus; so are, in varying degrees, pulpits, lecterns, reading desks, Bibles, flags, flowers, paintings, and even choirs! This does not mean that all are appropriate foci for worship. Some convey a contemporary meaning and should be retained, many have lost their former relevance, still others never really possessed any genuine significance. Good taste, an appreciation of the proper role of tradition, and sensitivity to the needs of contemporary worship should result in the retention of only those things which will have continued meaning and significance.

The Table/Altar

In this book we have interchangeably used the word table, or altar, or table/altar, to refer to the place from which Holy Communion, or the Eucharist, is celebrated. The history of the table/altar is complex and important. There seems little doubt that the early church celebrated the Eucharist around a common table, in the manner of the Last Supper. Beginning with the third century or thereabouts, a custom developed of holding the sacramental meal on the tombs of martyrs in the cemeteries or in the catacombs, and after Constantine this association of Holy Communion with deceased martyrs was almost universal. Relics were placed in stone coffins, and in the West these "coffin tables" gradually replaced the early wooden communion tables.

With the decline of congregational worship during the Middle Ages, the coffin altars became repositories for all sorts of things. Candles made their appearance on the altar, as did the tabernacle for the consecrated elements, containers for various relics, and the cross. Eventually the altar was pushed against the back wall, and from the late Middle Ages through the seventeenth century, the shrine grew to an immense size, while the people were situated far off and shielded from the altar by a screen.

After the Reformation there was an attempt to return to the practices of the early Christians in the observation of Holy Communion. In some churches the altar was replaced by a table that was brought forward, with the worshipers also coming forward to receive the elements while standing on three sides of the table. In some churches of Holland and Scotland, pews were removed from the nave for communion and replaced with tables so that each communicant could actually sit in a re-enactment of the Last Supper. In other places, communion was received by the people while seated in the pews, thus re-enacting the Last Supper but without the logistical problem of seating people at tables.

While altar rails were not unknown, the altar as a rule was unprotected by a rail until the 17th century. The first altar rail was installed probably to protect the altar from careless and irreverent treatment when it was not in use. William Laud, a 17th-century Archbishop of Canterbury, had some strong convictions on the placement of the altar, and, partly as a result of his influence, the communion table was pushed against the back wall and given a new emphasis by installing protective railings and gates. Since it was no longer convenient for the clergy to serve the elements to the people in their seats, it soon became customary for communicants to come forward and kneel at the railing.

During the 19th and first half of the 20th century, American Protestantism has been in considerable confusion about the place and importance of communion, and nowhere is this more evident than in the church buildings of the time. In churches affected by the revivalist movement, the communion table became an insignificant article of furniture tucked away in front of the platform on which the preacher and the choir played the main roles in the drama of worship. Elsewhere the table/altar assumed more and more the characteristics of a shrine, lodged against the far wall, well protected from the worshiping congregation by flowers, flags, candles, choir, and clergy. Other churches attempted to "beautify" their places of worship by installing shrinelike altars in buildings that were not designed initially to include such altars.

One of the results of the liturgical movement within both the Catholic and Protestant churches has been the recovery of meaning for the communion table. There are still differences among the various denominations, but the tendency is to restore the table/altar as a table, rather than use it as a repository for everything from money to flowers. Many are beginning to find a new beauty in a table that is well designed, simply built, adequately placed, and used only for the service of Holy Communion.

It is easy for the architect of a Protestant church to slip into a careless approach to theology in designing and locating the communion table. The table is a *symbol* of Christ in the congregation and the place around which the church gathers for the celebration of his sacrament. But it is not Christ, however, nor does it contain Christ. Architect E. A. Sövik has made the necessary distinction:

Among the Christians who do not believe in transubstantiation or in the reservation of the Host, care ought to be taken to avoid the impression that the altar is the seat or focus of God's presence. Shrine-like chancels have no congruity with evangelical Christianity. God is Spirit and He is where His people are. It seems reasonable that whatever is done in a church to support this concept is proper, and whatever is done to suggest that God's presence is more real in one location than another is a misrepresentation.[8]

The worship committee should carefully describe the place of the communion table in worship, and the architect should faithfully interpret the committee's intention. A strong design will help ensure that the table be one of the foci of worship. Visibility is needed, but Peter Hammond has rightly warned—apropos of Coventry Cathedral —that an altar can be so large as to become ridiculous.[9] A table, after all, is for people and should be scaled accordingly.

The location of the table in relationship to other foci of worship is equally important. The varying emphases placed on the Eucharist again need to be kept in mind; where communion is celebrated weekly, it *may* be defensible to design and place the communion table so that it dominates everything else, but the same table would be wrong for a church that celebrates communion only quarterly. Even within the churches that have historically placed a greater emphasis on communion than on any other liturgical act, there is a growing concern that the table should be properly related to those other major foci of Christian worship—the pulpit and baptismal font. Balance and proportion, however, do not necessarily mean putting the table in the middle, with font on one side and pulpit on the other! The question is: How can the architect design a building so that the implications of all aspects of worship are given full recognition?

A Place for Preaching of the Word

A place of worship must also provide an adequate place for the preaching of God's Word. To most people, this immediately suggests a pulpit, but it is well to remember that preaching is not dependent on the existence of a pulpit. A sermon may be given anywhere, and the worship committee has not completed its task until it has considered the full implications of setting aside a definite place for the preaching of the Word. As in all the inquiries of this committee, the first question is not where to put the pulpit, but, rather: What is preaching and what is its place in corporate worship?

Some people look on preaching as simply a human activity, a kind of teaching or instruction. Others see it as proclamation, the unfolding of the Word of God. As one theologian has written:

The Divine Word is not, however, present *ex opere operato;* preaching rather expresses God's freedom to speak his word, as and when he will, and the faith that for this he uses the instrumentality of men. The word of the preacher is not, therefore, any the less a human word, the word of a particular man to a particular congregation. It is intensely personal, and requires not that a man empty himself of his own personality, but that he speak (with seriousness and boldness) only as he in all honesty is able to discern for himself the truth of scripture, with the realisation that still he may be mistaken.[10]

Considered in this light, preaching and sacraments are inextricably woven together: "Word and Sacrament are only different media for the same reality, Christ's coming into the midst of his people." [11] Such awareness is not demonstrated by a pulpit placed in an insignificant corner of a large room, or by those that completely pre-empt the room for worship. The ideal is for the pulpit to be clearly related both spatially and visually to places reserved for the celebration of the sacraments.

To be effective, a solution requires an understanding of preaching on the part of the congregation. Many churchgoers apparently see little difference between preaching and old-fashioned oratory; others probably confuse it with a college lecture on religion. An orator depends on his ability to stir up an emotional response in his listeners, but he really has little in common with them. Preaching, on the other hand, is by one who is also a member of the community to which he preaches. He should be able to assume that the people will listen in an attitude of expectancy and will respond to what is being said. This is far from suggesting that the congregation will always accept what the preacher says, but the congregation has no right to reject what is preached simply because it is disturbing. The relationship between preacher and congregation is based on a mutual respect that still admits the possibility of conflict. Preaching is more than a lecture or a monologue; it does not exploit its listeners, but neither should it leave them indifferent. It is conversation in which the community responds by listening for the Word of God to be spoken.

These principles require that the pulpit be related visually and spatially to the places provided for the sacraments of Holy Communion and Baptism. Its size, location, and design should indicate the importance of preaching in worship, without rendering other important aspects of worship insignificant. The needs of people to see and hear should be respected; the height of the pulpit should be appropriate to the role that preaching plays in worship, never requiring the speaker to resort to oratorical techniques to communicate his insights. The basic concern in choosing a location for the pulpit is to foster a genuine relationship among the listeners and with the preacher.

Requirements for Baptism

Virtually all Christians affirm that Baptism is a sacrament, and Protestants characteristically say that it is one of only two sacraments. Protestant church buildings, however, either ignore Baptism altogether or treat it in a cavalier and incidental manner.

Unless the pastor and committee on worship rethink the importance of this sacrament, the architect will not receive adequate criteria for the design and placement of the baptismal font. For example: Is Baptism the infusion of God's grace by means of the priest, without involving the congregation at all, or is it the dedication of parents who covenant with God to raise the child in the Christian life? Or is it the act of the congregation in accepting the child into the Christian community, an acceptance that will later be confirmed by the covenant of the child when he is able to make the decision in his own behalf? Or is it the covenant of a person who voluntarily enters into a relationship with God and His Church, dying to the world and being raised to a new life of faith and obedience? Is the congregation a necessary part of Baptism or can it take place just as well in a side room, or in a hospital, or the family living room? May only an ordained clergyman perform the act or does the clergyman function simply in behalf of the congregation? When these questions are not faced, decisions are based on historical recollections, the personal preferences of the architect, or mere chance.

Some churches have tried to deal with this problem theologically and liturgically. One has placed its pulpit, table, and font at a place of maximum visibility so that the Word can be preached and both Communion and Baptism celebrated by the entire worshiping community. Another church has substituted the font for the lectern, expressing an appropriate relationship with the table and pulpit. In some churches that use immersion for Baptism, the tank is in full view, thus suggesting that the Baptism is an act of the whole congregation.

More frequently, however, churches use fonts that resemble bird baths more than places for Christian Baptism,[12] or put such emphasis on chubby naked babies that the sacrament is reduced to gurgles during the ceremony. A congregation betrays a poverty of understanding if it is more responsive to the baby's clothing than to the realities of grace, thanksgiving, and covenant.

As much as the communion table and the pulpit, the design of the baptismal font should be integrally related to belief. If the font is nothing more than a repository for water, with some decorative elements added, responsibility lies primarily in the failure of the worship committee to convey its concepts to the architect.

Some churches and architects have selected a location for the font after studying where it was placed centuries ago. In the Middle Ages, a baptistry was usually located at or near the front entrance of the church, or, if no baptistry was provided, the font was often placed at the front entryway. This was meant to signify a person's entrance into the church by Baptism, and, in terms of medieval theology, this was a rational solution. However, for a church that places great emphasis on the community of faith and its involvement in the observance of the sacraments, such a location is not only awkward but denies the congregation any opportunity to participate in the rite. Since participation is considered part of the celebration of the sacrament, the font should be located where it can serve as a focus of congregational attention and concern. In any case, no responsible committee can ignore Baptism in the design of the place of worship; if it is truly a sacrament, it is entitled to recognition in the space provided for the congregation to meet as a worshiping body.

Little has been said concerning the large group of churches that baptize by immersion in a pool located in or adjacent to the place of worship, but they are usually the ones with the clearest understanding of what they believe concerning Baptism. Here the problem is primarily architectural—how to provide a place for immersion that is in proper proportion to the rest of the room and permits the congregation to share in the sacrament as a community of faith, not simply act as observers at a private ritual. There are also functional problems, such as providing access for the minister from the worship room to the pool and a way by which persons to be baptized may leave the congregation and go to dressing rooms.

Providing for the Reading of the Word

Every place of worship should have a place from which the Bible can be read and the reading heard by the worshiping congregation. The reading of the Word has been viewed in several ways. Historically, in the highly liturgical churches the unordained layman was often permitted to read the Word, but he could not do so from the pulpit, which was reserved for the clergy. In the reformed churches the absolute distinction between clergy and laymen was blurred; the latter were often used not only to read, but, on occasion, to preach and expound the meaning of the Word. Predictably, in those churches that customarily barred laymen from the pulpit, ambos, lecterns, and reading desks naturally evolved. It is more difficult to understand how other churches that did not place this emphasis on the difference in role between clergy and laity could develop these same accouterments of worship.

For example, in some churches the use of the lectern can be traced to the shortage of ministers after the Reformation. To alleviate this shortage, lay readers were used to lead some services. A reader's desk, or "lattron," was improvised as the place for the lay reader, who was not permitted to enter the pulpit to preach the Word. In the Anglican church, the use of the reader's desk is derived from the custom of reading the lessons in the nave as distinguished from the chancel, which was reserved for the Eucharist.

In other churches there are no such explanations for the use of the lectern, which was revived in the nineteenth century out of a desire to imitate medieval building styles. Since that time it has had a popular place in the design of many Protestant churches, but more as a device for balancing the chancel furniture than out of regard for theology or liturgy. Today's practice is often to use the lectern for prayers and reading of the Scriptures, while reserving the pulpit for preaching. A number of contemporary critics argue that the reading of the Word and its preaching are part of the same liturgical act, and that for a church to divide these functions is to do violence both to theology and liturgy.

As with other matters, the church's decision in regard to the inclusion of a lectern should be on the basis of function and belief.

The location of the Bible is intimately related to a decision on the lectern. If the lectern is to be used as a place for reading the Scriptures, then the lectern is the logical place for the Bible. If the Bible is to be read from the pulpit, that is where it should be. Placing the Bible on the altar or table, however, seems to make the Bible an object of veneration or imply that it possesses magical qualities.

The "Choir Problem"

Congregational hymn singing has always played an important part in Protestant worship, and since Vatican Council II it has taken on an increased role in Catholic services. Every church building should be suitable not only for hymn singing, but its acoustical qualities ought to encourage a maximum singing response by everyone present. To stand and attempt to sing in a sound-dead church, where the only voices you hear are those of the choir, your own, and perhaps that of the person next to you is disheartening and destructive.

Few worship committees would disagree with these conclusions, but as soon as the problem of the choir is raised, controversy seems inevitable. For one thing, acoustics that are ideal for the choir very often are too "alive" for preaching. Either the choir accepts slightly deadened acoustics or the reverberations of the minister's voice may stun the congregation. Choir anthems have become a treasured tradition in most churches, and yet it is difficult for a choir to sing an anthem without seeming to be performing artists. Placing choirs in rear galleries produces excellent tonal results, but most congregations have great difficulty restraining their desire to turn and look at those who are singing.

To complicate matters, choir directors are usually so awkwardly positioned in relation to the choir and the congregation that either the elaborate gestures of the choir master are dominant or he is concealed from the congregation and can function only with the help of unsightly mirrors. Divided choirs possess geometrical balance, but their function seems lost in an age when antiphonal responses are rarely heard.

The penchant of some congregations for multiple choirs (a church near Pittsburgh has places for five!), the desire of congregation and clergy for self-aggrandizing colorful processionals, singers who wish to give formal recitals periodically, the need for robing rooms and practice rooms, and the demand of many congregations that the choir be visible when they sing but somehow drop out of sight when they are finished—such complications make it easy to understand why churches have never ceased to experiment with the location of the choir.

Although the practice of using singers, especially in the larger churches, had been accepted for many centuries, choirs were not usually found in parish churches until the middle of the 1800s. Two powerful religious movements of that time—revivalism and the Cambridge movement with its emphasis on the glory of medieval Christendom—found important roles for the choir to play. The revivalists used the choir to help lead church meetings, and emphasized its importance by locating the choir on the platform with the preacher. Churches intrigued with worship as it was viewed in the Middle Ages saw the choir as an ideal solution for long, empty chancels. The pageantry which the choir made possible, coupled with the aesthetically satisfactory placement of the choir in the divided chancel, struck a popular note. It was not long before every church either featured a choir seated in a split chancel or one that was proudly perched in front, alongside, or above the preacher. In one case, a misguided theological concept placed the choir in the chancel; in the other, pure functionalism moved the choir forward and put it in a place of prominence.

This situation, which has prevailed with some variations until recent years, represents a serious problem; few people seem to understand the important role the choir can play in worship. It is not a question of Shall we have a choir? but rather, How can we provide the choir a place in our church that is not only theologically correct and consistent with our beliefs but is also technically appropriate for their talents?

A satisfactory architectural solution of the "choir problem" requires objective and insightful analysis of what the choir is and what it can and should do in the service of worship. Some have suggested that the choir's task is to create a musical effect in much the same way as lighting and color create visual effects. It is true that the words of the music are frequently unintelligible—indeed, some of our greatest religious music is in a foreign language—but this understanding of "effect" unfairly limits the potential of music, which is capable of doing much more than stirring emotions. Others have emphasized the choir's responsibility to lead congregational singing. In practice, however, the choir tends to supplant rather than to lead congregational singing, although it can certainly perform a significant service in this area. Sometimes the choir's role is described as a participation in the ministry of the Word, along with preaching and the reading of Scripture. If this is true, greater concern should be exercised for the texts of some of the anthems that churches frequently use. Under some circumstances the choir could join in the service in such a way that their contribution is the equivalent of preaching, but, practically speaking, this is not the normal or expected result. A choir is not just a group of talented singers, an accouterment of worship, or something to cover the "awkward" period of the service when the offering is collected. Theologically, the choir should be considered as part of a response by which the congregation expresses its praise, adoration, and gratitude. This would indicate a need for restraint, lest its enthusiasm for responding on behalf of the congregation supplant all congregational singing!

The architectural solutions have been so varied that it is hard to think of a location that has not been tried. Churches have placed choirs in split chancels; behind the minister on a platform; behind the minister but hidden by a screen; on platforms ascending and descending (the choir is out of sight except when singing); off to one side of the chancel, both exposed and hidden; in a transept or simulated transept; in front of, in the middle, and at the back of the congregation; in a side gallery, back gallery, and gallery over the chancel. Although none of these "answers" is completely satisfactory, in deciding on location of the choir, several principles should be kept in mind:

1. The importance of the table/altar, pulpit, or font must not be reduced, or their roles confused.
2. There should be clear recognition that the choir is of the congregation, not separate from it.
3. The choir's response in music is to be the congregation's response to God.
4. The functional requirements of singing—such as the necessity for a director to be close to the source of accompanying music, and for the choir to be heard by the congregation—cannot be ignored.

Choirs also need a place to hang robes, store music, and rehearse. Since many choirs like to have a "warm-up practice" just before the service begins, it is wise to locate the practice room where it can be used for that purpose. The architect and building committee will also want to study the route the choir will have to follow in going from the rehearsal and robing rooms to its place in a processional or choir stall.

Music in the Church

It does not require an Old Testament prophet to predict with some confidence the course of church music during the next decade. The signs are all about us that contemporary popular music will soon be felt strongly within the churches. The jazz masses of Ed Summerlin and Roger Ortmayer in the late '50s were only the beginning of "experimental" music in worship services. In actuality, the word experimental is inaccurate. The folk, rock, and jazz forms which are now being used with increasing frequency are experimental only in that the traditional classical organ music is supplemented or in some cases displaced by music created by instruments which heretofore have not customarily been used in church services. As the youth of today become the tastemakers of tomorrow, the kinds of church music forms to which this generation responds will multiply and become increasingly acceptable within the church.

Church building committees should be acutely aware of these developments. Worship spaces, in particular, should be so designed that a variety of musical instruments can be accommodated, whether they be "newly discovered" harpsichords, drums, electric guitars, or other contemporary innovations. It is doubtful, however, whether the organ will ever lose its pre-eminence or be replaced by the new sounds of this generation. The most swinging person of the younger set often responds with equal enthusiasm to Bach, and no instrument has yet been invented which can more fully reveal the genius and creativity of such a composer.

Those who opt for an organ in the place of worship will want to spend a great deal of time evaluating the various organs available. The architect should be involved in these discussions as there are a number of related architectural problems: the location of the organ with reference to the choir and congregation, its visual impact on the place of worship, acoustics, and similar matters. If the committee avoids unilateral action, the architect can contribute valuable counsel and information; indeed, the success of the building will to some degree depend on the architectural solutions in this area.

Many building committees are faced with the difficult decision of whether the organ should be a pipe organ or an electronic instrument.

Electronic organs have vastly improved in recent years, but it is worth noting that they are almost always promoted in terms of how much they sound like a pipe organ. All things being equal, a pipe organ would seem to be preferable. If a church cannot afford an instrument that costs more than a few thousand dollars, a decision to buy an electronic organ may be warranted, but the idea of using a good piano until an organ can be purchased might well be considered. Furthermore, the difference in cost between an adequate pipe organ and an electronic instrument is less than is commonly assumed.

One of the factors affecting cost is the mistaken notion of some churches that the organ they purchase must have the versatility required for concert recitals. Except for a few churches, the purpose of an organ is to provide music for worship, including musical accompaniment for the choir and congregation. A church whose first concern is quality rather than versatility can often acquire a pipe organ that satisfies all its needs for no more money than it was prepared to spend on an electronic instrument.

Another misconception haunting many building committees is that there is something aesthetically or theologically wrong with exposed organ pipes. It is true that one of the arguments frequently advanced against the Akron and auditorium plans drew attention to this feature, but the real objection to these buildings was their aesthetic deficiency. For example, most of the visible pipes were false, painted with curlicues, and located in such a way that they seemed only an expression of congregational pride. Pipes that pretentiously call attention to themselves reflect a superficial understanding of worship. Exposed in a natural and unassuming way, however, they not only enhance the quality of music but can play a major role in creating an aesthetically satisfying place for worship.

Because pipes are so dominant, churches and architects should be cautious about placing them in the front of the building. While there is no rule that applies in all situations, rear galleries often make excellent locations, and a side position toward the front of the worship room can sometimes be most satisfactory. The decision as to where to place the choir will also affect the placement of the pipes; the choir should be located close enough to the emission of sound to avoid the problem of a disconcerting time lag.

The "Human Factor" in Church Design

Churches are for people—although many buildings would cause one to doubt it. Even when they have chancels, splendid naves, and beautiful furnishings, they are frequently not well designed for people to use them. Perhaps the parking lot is not convenient to the entrance, or stairs may present problems for persons with physical limitations. The pews may be very uncomfortable for sitting, or be so arranged that a person cannot see and hear everything that is taking place.

Many things can be done if a church is concerned for people. For example, a church will take into account people's physical infirmities, providing ways in which those who are crippled or suffer other physical disabilities can enter without calling undue attention to themselves. At least one entrance should be designed so that, if necessary, people can be deposited at an entryway and proceed immediately to a seat without climbing stairs or traversing steep ramps. Once inside the church, the rooms and passageways should not add unnecessarily to the difficulty such a person has in getting from place to place.

Are Pews Really Needed?

The seating provided for worshipers deserves careful consideration. Although in the medieval period, for example, the congregation was expected to stand or perhaps sit on the floor, today we tend to think of pews as traditional. They may lend a certain tone to a building, but they are not always desirable, since fixed pews freeze the use of space to a single purpose. Some of the new churches of Europe have had considerable success in introducing finely designed chairs instead of pews, thus preserving greater flexibility in the use of space.

Pews should not be installed in a room that is being used temporarily for worship but will have other functions when the master plan is completed. Purchasing pews for a temporary worship building is not only extravagant but offers an unfortunate temptation to use them later in the permanent place for worship, even though they may not fit properly or be of suitable design. It is even worse to install "temporarily" in the new building pews that were used in the old building;

it would be far better to use chairs "temporarily." The total effect of many good buildings has been impaired by the specious assumption that a place of worship must have pews and that any pews will do.

Since seating arrangement is an integral part of the design, the furnishings, including pews, should be purchased in consultation with the architect, or better yet, they should be designed by him. The architect is surely entitled to a major voice in deciding what will best serve the building he has designed.

Seating arrangements should not only be compatible with the design but comfortable as well. Adequate space should be allowed between rows so that people can move easily in from the aisle, and it must be kept in mind that seating is difficult if rows are inordinately long. Pew-ends should not be used unless there are sound reasons for doing so, as they hinder the movement of people entering and leaving. The kind of back provided by the pew or chair should be tested to see if it fits a variety of human shapes and sizes. A committee might well sit for thirty or forty minutes in pews similar to those being proposed to see how comfortable they are after that length of time. Storage must be provided for hymn books, communion glasses, and other items. Finally, a protective screen is needed for the front pew, since, otherwise, people intuitively avoid it.

Places for Private Meditation—Chapels and Their Use

This chapter has emphasized the importance of a place for public worship and the necessity of thinking of worship in terms broader than individual experience. But there are times when public worship is not enough, and there is need to withdraw for private mediation. This may occur when people are at home, or at work, and also at odd times and places that cannot be predicted. Catholics attempt to meet this need by keeping their churches open, but few Protestant churches have a place where people can come to worship unobtrusively any time of day or night and then leave without explanation. Some churches have provided chapels, with easy access to the street and with little risk of damage or desecration. A chapel need not be large; it can have seats for perhaps no more than seventy-five or one hundred, and can be simply and economically furnished. Plans for a chapel are commonly included in a master plan, but few are actually built. Unfortunately, the chapel idea usually develops out of sentiment or as a memorial to one or more persons, rather than out of a concern to meet the need for private worship.

It is far better for a church not to include a chapel as a "must" but to determine its program requirements in the light of its understanding of the needs for places to worship and the mission to be accomplished. The truth is that many chapels are gathering dust for lack of use, usually as the result of being erected without a clear understanding as to what their purpose should be. Inappropriately located or inadequately arranged either for weddings or funerals, they are frequently so tied into the church building complex that they cannot even be used for private worship, and stand as unhappy monuments to sentimental churchmanship.

Finally, a brief comment should be made concerning the conviction of those persons, apparently growing in number, that worship as we have known it within many Protestant churches must undergo radical revision and updating.

Potentially, worship stands as one of the most powerful experiences men can know, yet each Sunday morning hundreds of empty pews testify that many people assign a higher priority to other activities. Perhaps there was a time when a new sanctuary could serve as a strong drawing card, but it is doubtful that, at least in any substantial number of churches, such will be the case again.

The problem is that worship, to have meaning, must express life and one's response to the gift of life, and often our worship fails to do this. It is here that so much needs to be done, not only to lighten the intolerable weight of some traditional forms of worship, but to find new ways to relate worship to the concerns of life. If this is done, then a new building will prove invaluable. But unless new life is breathed into the bones of dead worship patterns, no building, regardless of its beauty, design, and arrangements, can fill the void that seems to exist.

---◦◄ ❋ ►◦---

CHAPTER TEN

Space, Form, and Christian Education

> "The congestion of the peak-hour Sunday morning schedule
> combined with the high hourly costs of contemporary church buildings
> may force the church of tomorrow to move away from Sunday school
> and toward Christian education." [1]
>
> —*Lyle E. Schaller*

Christian educators of all persuasions are taking a new look at the educational ministry of the church. Old concepts that placed a heavy emphasis on learning the facts and teachings of the Bible are being replaced by new approaches that recognize that Christian education begins with a concern for persons. Roger Shinn argues that Christian education is more than teaching people "all *about* Christianity," and is not "simply a business of pumping information into people's heads." Rather, "It is inviting them to share the common life of Christians." [2] In its simplest terms, Christian education is the introduction of persons into the life and mission of the community of Christian faith.

Christian education, therefore, means a concern for *all* people, not just the young. Far more than teaching young people facts about the Christian faith, its task is to nurture persons so that they can become effective members of the community of faith. It ultimately encompasses the entire teaching and learning life of the congregation.

Such an approach implies a great deal about the buildings to be erected. A Christian education committee can no longer be satisfied with listing age groups by number and class, and specifying the number of square feet that will be needed for each class, however important such information may be. The committee must begin by asking what needs to be done to carry out the task of Christian education and what space will be required to accomplish this result. On the basis of this analysis, church and architect should be able to determine the specific requirements for Christian education.

The authoritative and indispensable work for every church engaged in building educational facilities is *Focus: Building for Christian Education* by Mildred C. Widber and Scott T. Ritenour.[3] The present chapter is not a substitute for their book, but is conceived as introductory and supplemental to it. In their book, Ritenour and Widber have described the concern of Christian education for such questions as how people grow, the forces that cause personality to become what it is, the process of maturation (including the development of one's religious life), and the special needs of old age. They have emphasized that Christian education cannot be considered at an end when a person is confirmed or when he graduates from high school; otherwise, a whole catalog of needs will have been ignored.

Recognition of a wide range of needs, however, does not mean that every need requires a separate room. Some can be met adequately by using community facilities or the homes of parishioners. The committee's responsibility is to do the necessary homework so that needed space is provided, and to ensure that no vital concern is thoughtlessly disregarded because of an inability to see beyond traditional classroom requirements.

Relationship of Christian Education to Worship

There is an obvious and close relationship between Christian education and the church at worship, but this has been understood in many different, and sometimes unfortunate, ways. A few years ago, it was fashionable to gather the young people for "opening exercises," a facsimile of the adult worship service, after which they were dispersed to their classrooms. In fact, one of the purposes of the Akron-style church building was to provide a convenient place for this format.

Today, one fairly common solution is the "family service," in which young people attend an early service timed to coincide with the church school. After a hymn, sometimes an anthem by a junior choir, scripture, and "junior sermon," the young people retire to their classrooms for instruction.

In other churches, one or more chapels are installed throughout the education building, where worship services are conducted in much the same fashion as "opening exercises," although they are frequently more elaborate and ritualistic. Some congregations build "worship centers" in each classroom, with the expectation that each class will worship during the class session. These centers are sometimes facsimile altars that are tucked away in a cabinet when not needed, or they may be built as a part of the permanent furniture in the classrooms, or may be simple tables with flowers, cross, candles, and the like.

Each of these solutions is subject to serious criticism. The "opening exercises" tend to become routine and meaningless. Also, it is difficult to see how today's young people would find the usual "family service" a meaningful worship experience, and church-school chapels have encouraged an adult-centered ritual that tends to be unrelated to the needs of young people. As to classroom worship, there are theological questions to be raised concerning the typical altars employed; some have serious reservations about having so many altars. Of course, answers have been offered to these objections, but it can fairly be said that many Christian education committees do not stop to consider the theological implications of some traditional church-school practices. Many denominations have given careful thought to worship as it relates to education, and building committees should seek out denominational recommendations before finalizing the building program.

The paradox is that a separation of the worshiping congregation from the education ministry might well result in drawing these two aspects of the church's life into a closer relationship For example, instead of structured, planned worship services for young people, it might be better Christian education to place the emphasis on providing a variety of experiences and imparting a body of knowledge, on the assumption that persons so engaged will sometimes worship together when the circumstances suggest that there is a common need and desire. In this way worship would occur as a correlative of the task they are dealing with rather than as a stylized service in a formal setting. Worship that is related to common experiences is often not only more meaningful, but it is also an excellent basis on which to develop patterns that will eventually be reflected in the quality of worship experienced by the whole congregation.

Commonly Accepted Square-Footage Recommendations

It is surprising how often a building committee—or an architect—will decide that a teaching ministry calls for a specified number of square feet, and will then proceed to divide a building into equal-sized rooms. Since young people have different needs at different ages, such a division will inevitably mean that some rooms are too crowded, while others are not used to full capacity. A building study report should specify the various kinds of rooms that will be required, and the architect's preliminary drawings ought to indicate how the proposed building will meet specific needs—that is, what space is allocated for preschool children, for teenagers, etc. Nevertheless, in such specialized planning there is a danger that the rooms cannot be adapted for future uses at a reasonable cost. Space should be designed for function, but not be so frozen that desirable changes are economically or structurally impossible.

The recommendations of Widber and Ritenour for minimum needs at each age level are summarized in the following chart. Of course, building committees should refer to their book for the reasoning behind the recommendations; the chart is offered simply as a check list to determine whether the written program of the Christian education building committee meets acceptable standards.

These standards must be considered tentative, as the needs and exigencies of individual situations may require a church to vary from the precise recommendations. However, they have been approved by most denominations and validated by experience, and thus a church should hesitate to depart from them except when a variation is clearly indicated.

Spatial Qualities Which Are Needed

The Christian education building committee has the broad responsibility of dealing with the varieties of uses and needs included in

AGE GROUP STANDARDS IN

Age Group	Maximum Children Per Room	Floor Space Per Child	Toilets and Drinking Facilities	Space for Wraps
TODDLERS Ages 1½–2	8–12	35 sq. ft.	Should be adjoining room with small fixtures.	Rod with hangers *in* the room 2½ ft. from floor. (Full-length space for teachers.)
NURSERY CLASS	15–18	35 sq. ft.	Same as above.	*In* the room 3 ft. from floor.
KINDER-GARTEN	20	30–35 sq. ft.	Same as above.	*In* the room 3½ ft. from floor.
PRIMARY Grades 1 and 2	16–25	25–30 sq. ft.	Separate for boys and girls. On same floor.	In room preferably. 3½–4 ft. from floor.

BUILDING AND BASIC EQUIPMENT*

Storage Space	Equipment	Chairs	Tables
Ample storage space for supplies. Low open shelves for children's toys, etc. Preferably movable.	Clean, warm floor with plastic, rubber, or asphalt tile. Large, soft, washable rug.	6" from floor. Only 5 or 6 are needed.	16" high. (All table tops 10" higher than chair seats.) Top surfaces approx. 18" x 24". Only 1 or 2 tables needed.
Closet with door for teachers' supplies and wraps.	Tackboard on eye level of child.		
Same as above. Consider size of pictures for filing space and open shelves of various widths to allow for blocks and varied objects.	Same as above. Rug large enough for children to sit on during group time.	8" from floor.	18" high, 24" x 36". Beware of filling space with tables! Open floor space is great need for this age.
Same as above	Same as above.	Some 10", some 12" from floor.	20" high, some 30" x 36", some 24" x 36". Smaller tables as above preferable. Beware of too many tables. Open floor space is needed.
Storage space for teachers' and pupils' supplies; file for varied sized pictures; open shelves for children's books, larger objects, wall space for murals, etc.	Adequate tackboard and chalkboard at eye level on 1 or 2 sides of room. Piano desirable. Record player desirable.	Some 12", some 14" from floor.	24" high, 30" x 48". Round table for reading corner; small rectangular table for worship center. Arrange so there is open floor space for activities such as informal dramatic presentations, games, singing, etc.

AGE GROUP STANDARDS IN

Age Group	Maximum Children Per Room	Floor Space Per Child	Toilets and Drinking Facilities	Space for Wraps
LOWER JUNIOR Grades 3 and 4	16–25	25–30 sq. ft.	Preferably on same floor as above.	In room preferably. 4–4½ ft. from floor.
JUNIOR Grades 5 and 6	25	25–30 sq. ft.	Preferably on same floor as room.	In room preferably. 4–4½ ft. from floor.

Christian education. It is inescapably involved with the needs of several different age levels. Thus, one of its major questions is: How should these differences be reflected in the qualities of space provided? Not only do space and room arrangements for three- and four-year-old children differ markedly from requirements for youths or older people, but the specifications for a building may also be affected by the environmental background of those to be served. Many people will not respond in a learning atmosphere that is vastly different from what they know in their homes, schools, and places of employment. This is not to insist that the church duplicate secular environment, but simply to indicate that the church cannot provide an atmosphere so much at variance with what is familiar that an insurmountable barrier is erected.

Some lessons derived from experience merit consideration. Rooms planned for three-, four-, and five-year-olds should say, "Come—Look —Do—Make—Try New Things—Make New Friends," and several places in the room should express the wonder of living. There are describable methods of planning the space, grouping, and equipment to make freedom of movement and activities possible, but it is impossible to find a formula that would ensure the desired atmosphere of kindness, acceptance, and, perhaps, adventure.

Warm and inviting colors and rooms that recognize the need for physical comfort and lend themselves easily to a variety of arrangements are surely appropriate for the six-to-eleven group. Space areas conducive

BUILDING AND BASIC EQUIPMENT *(cont'd)*

Storage Space	Equipment	Chairs	Tables
Same as primary, with space for maps, large pictures, large objects.	Same as primary, plus access to filmstrip or movie projector.	Some 14", some 15" from floor.	24" and 25" high—same as above for reading and worship. Arrange so there is open floor space for varied activities.
Same as lower junior and primary	Same as lower junior	16" from floor.	26" high, 30" x 48" as above for reading, library, and worship.

to conversation, storytelling, and such teaching activities as dramatics, painting, and role-playing should be included.

The rooms for older young people should be conducive to group study, discussion, and related activities. Again it is psychologically important that the rooms be fresh and modern in their colors, furnishings, use of light, and arrangements. Nothing inhibits the use of a room more than an impression of over-all unimaginative dullness. In general, the qualities of the rooms should be related to the personalities and needs of those who are to use them; this is equally true in planning for older people, where a bit of conservatism might well be in order. A church need not look the same throughout. What is important is that the spaces provided relate intelligently to the educational program of the church.

Perhaps the most important principle for an education committee is that, if education is part of the religious life of the community, buildings for this purpose should be designed so they are visually, architecturally, and psychologically an integral part of a whole.

This is perhaps best illustrated by reflecting on how often we speak of the Christian education building as the "educational wing." Since most education facilities are designed in such a manner that they appear to be "hooked on" to the worship building, which in turn is given architectural emphasis, the phrase most accurately describes many education units. The distinct separation from the rest of the church can

AGE GROUP STANDARDS IN

7TH THROUGH 12TH

Age Group	Maximum Children Per Room	Floor Space Per Child	Furniture and Equipment
Grades 7–8	15–20	15–18 sq. ft.	When a junior or senior high group of 15–20 or 25 meets in one room, it is assumed that for part of the time they will be in smaller interest groups working on varied teaching-learning activities. Thus, one group of 5 or 6 might be working on a map; another of 8 or 10 could be working out a dramatic choric speech; while a 3d would be working on a dramatic skit. Each group might have an adult guide. Together this same group might view and discuss a movie or filmstrip; listen to a resource person who has something of special interest to contribute to the ongoing study-project. Obviously, then, any room for these young persons must allow for flexibility of arrangement, i.e., space for movement. For that reason *15–18 sq. ft. is not too much floor space for each person.*
Grades 9–10	15–20	15–18 sq. ft.	
Grades 11–12	25	15–18 sq. ft.	

* Prepared by Mildred Widber and adapted from *Building for Christian Education*, published by the Board of Christian Education of the United Presbyterian Church, U.S.A. Used by permission.

cause young people, and older ones as well, to think of education as divorced from the main life and principal activity of the church. Young people especially begin to think of "their place" as opposed to adult areas. Since worship and education are part of the same mission, the

BUILDING AND BASIC EQUIPMENT *(cont'd)*
GRADES

Furniture and Equipment	Teachers and Leaders	Other Considerations
Colorful, attractive furnishings in keeping with décor of the building. Comfortable, sturdy chairs. Tables that can be used for work space when needed or pushed to one side when major floor space is needed. Folding tables could be considered if they are sturdy. There should be storage cabinets for study materials, pictures, hymnals, Bibles, and varied creative activities materials. Wall maps, display boards, a well-selected youth library which may be on open shelves, the tops to be used for display purposes, give a room a lived-in look. These groups should have access to a good record player, movie and filmstrip machines, screen, and audio-visual materials in keeping with their particular study project. This means electrical outlets should be carefully planned and placed. Cloak storage space and toilet facilities should be nearby. Consideration should be given to the need for recreation, handicraft and hobbies, dramatics, youth choirs, etc.	However and wherever youth groups meet, their teachers and leaders need every now and then to meet together, to plan together, and to know the general direction and goals for the total youth work in their particular church. For discussion groups, there should be a leader for every 8 or 10; for the larger group, one person may lead, although the other teachers in the group may assist or the teachers may rotate their leadership in the larger group.	Consideration should be given to the need for recreation, handicraft and hobbies, dramatics, youth choirs, etc. For some of these activities the all-purpose fellowship may be ideal.

unity of the two should be reflected architecturally in every possible way. Yet in fact the architectural statement of most buildings denies this unity.

The validity of this criticism can be confirmed by a casual examination of any book or article containing pictures of new churches. Most visitors—and photographers—confine their examination to the entrance way, the nave or worship unit, and the grounds. One architect, responding to a comment on the dullness of the educational facility, frankly replied, "What can you expect? They are just classrooms—and classrooms are classrooms." Perhaps the problem is largely that educational buildings have not been considered very important either by the architect or by churchmen. Such buildings have often been "tacked on," so to speak, in ways that say much about the program of the church and disparage its educational mission.

Similarly, many churches—and their architects—expend all their creativity designing a place for worship, but where education is concerned, they are willing to settle for unimaginative, repetitive spaces associated with run-of-the-mill public-school classrooms. Although in some communities extensive research and imaginative architecture have resulted in public schools that churches could well emulate, there is no need for carbon copies of standardized solutions which do not meet the needs of the church.

Problems Arising from Standardized Spaces

Specifying needs for a Christian education building in terms of square footage can pose a problem. Clearly, it is essential that a church have adequate space in which to teach. Not too many years ago it was necessary to convince congregations—and occasionally architects—that square footage and the size of rooms were important factors in carrying out a teaching program. However, minimum square-footage standards were accepted by many architects and denominational leaders in the mid-1950s, and these recommendations are still largely recognized as basic. Many of these recommendations are included in the chart on pages 112–117. Experience has shown that these standards are good ones, but they also tempt building committees and some architects to short-circuit the task of planning for Christian education. A building committee is discharging its duties superficially if it simply takes the square-footage recommendations, adds the appropriate numbers for each age group, and gives the tabulation to the architect as a statement of the church's education program. Guides originally developed to break open education spaces and provide more space for teaching activity have tended to encourage monotonous standardization. Thus, utilitarian function has become paramount over spatial qualities; the result is that we have few education buildings which reflect true creativity.

If the sole criterion is the number of square feet necessary for each age group, rooms tend to be standardized rectangles. This is an economical space divider, but an unthinking use of the rectangle creates an institutional atmosphere. "Look alike" rooms may be economical, but they are not usually the product of sensitive program planning. In building one's own home, for example, rooms would not be identical in shape. The architect would consider the activity projected for the individual rooms, the people who will live in them, their ages and tastes. Not only would obvious distinctions develop, but there would be subtle differences as well—such as window spacings, the amount of exterior light projected, the manner in which interior light is provided, variation in shapes and décor.

Multipurpose Facilities

The architect and building committee should plan for a maximum use of the education building from the beginning, with each room serving as many purposes as are practical. Simple economics dictates that the more use a room receives, the lower the cost per use for the building.

Traditionally, Christian education buildings have had a one-hour per week specialized use, representing an extraordinarily high cost per person. It would be wise for the appropriate committee to test its specifications for rooms in the light of the cost factor. For example, if an education building should cost $500,000 and the span of its usability is estimated to be thirty years, the yearly depreciation cost is $16,666 ($500,000 divided by 30). If other costs chargeable to the church school should total $5,000 annually (this is low, if the salary of a professional Christian education director is to be included), the total yearly cost of the church school will be approximately $21,666. Assuming an average attendance of two hundred for each Sunday of the year, the cost per use is $2.00 for each time a person attends the church school. If the average attendance is less, the cost per use will be higher; if the attendance is greater, the cost per use is lower. There are an infinite number of possible combined uses, and simple economics requires that building committees should explore all possible variations to assure maximum use.

Occasionally one sees signs that a church committee and architect tried to plan for various possibilities, but did not consider all of the ramifications of multiple use. For example: Is the furniture compatible with the different uses intended? Has adequate storage space been provided? Practical factors may make it unwise to require adults to use rooms sometimes occupied by small children. Intelligent multiple-use planning requires careful evaluation of everything involved in using the same place for two activities. It must be possible to schedule the activities at different times, and they must be compatible in the furnishings and equipment required.

One of the key emphases of this book is that church buildings should reflect the faith of the community, but it is much more difficult to realize this aim in the facilities for education than in the place of worship. There is a tradition and body of experience behind the design of the latter which provide a point of beginning. Nevertheless, the problem of building adequate educational facilities that do not become quickly outdated will not be solved until ways have been found to relate more satisfactorily the mission of Christian education and the architecture of its buildings.

Art and Education

Few churches seem to realize the role art can play in Christian education. Sometimes it seems to have a kind of "pin-up" function in church-school buildings, with vaguely decorative intentions. What is conveyed in this fashion is often strangely inappropriate—one church school, for example, has a hall picture of Ivanhoe being knighted by his king! Pictures used for the value of their "message" are often saying something quite at odds with what the church is trying to teach. The tasteless sentimentality of "Jesus art" is the most obvious distortion with which many churches indulge their fancies.

Even a great work of art will not please everyone, but this should not deter a church from exploring the possibilities of various art forms. Because of the complexity of the subject and the range of related problems, a church at the outset might entrust the selection to a specially chosen committee. Its members should be sensitive to the artist's point of view and also keep in mind that works of art appropriate in rooms set aside for young children will have different qualities than those selected for adults. The trite, the imitative, and the bizarre are to be rejected, which means that the judgments of the committee cannot be dictated by preconception or lack of understanding.

Much of the art in Christian education buildings offers a complacent and superficial understanding of faith, with the darkness and bitterness of the world eliminated. Art forms should reflect not just tranquillity and joy but the full spectrum of human feeling.

It is also possible for the church to elicit artistic responses from those who take part in its educational program; the results often have more meaning than any art work that might be commissioned. For example, the church school in the First Congregational Church of Vancouver, Washington, prepared a mosaic from tiny bits of stained glass salvaged from its former church building. The mosaic was prepared over a period of four months and placed in four panels. Imaginatively conceived, lovingly and carefully executed, it speaks to all ages of the wonders of God's creation. While this mosaic does not meet "professional standards," it is nevertheless a good example of art in the service of the church.

The architect, of course, ought to be involved in all the decisions relative to the commissioning or acquisition of a work of art for a new education building. The same criteria that were established for art in the place of worship apply with equal force here.

Experimentation in Christian Education

The steady progress of the ecumenical movement has many future implications for Christian education. Today every church is facing more or less the same kind of problem when it considers the economics of building for its education needs, and many churches share a common concern for the quality of the education program that can be financed after new buildings are erected. Practical as well as theological considerations will soon cause the major Protestant denominations, and perhaps the Catholic church and some Jewish groups, to find new ways in which they can work for common objectives in religious education.

One harbinger of the future is the co-operative project at Columbia, Maryland. In 1964, the Division of Christian Life and Mission of the

National Council of Churches voted to explore the possibilities of new forms of ecumenical ministries in this new town to be built midway between Washington and Baltimore. The Archdiocese of Baltimore, a number of Protestant denominations, and Jewish groups are at the time this is written engaged in joint planning for the religious life of this community, and, while it is too early to predict the success of this work, the progress thus far is encouraging.

Most of the ideas being tested and implemented at Columbia were derived from "working papers" prepared by Dr. Stanley J. Hallett. His radical and yet practical proposals have already had a major effect on the thinking of many religious groups. While the proposals cover a wide spectrum of possibilities, one of the principal recommendations calls for ecumenical co-operation in the creation of religious facilities. Dr. Hallett concludes among other things that, by constructing buildings for common usage, the major faiths can save enough money to pay for a relatively full schedule of classes and activities throughout the week, with a staff of professional religious educators. The report is an imaginative attack on the waste incurred when churches duplicate facilities that each church uses for very limited periods of time. While opportunities for ecumenical co-operation are not usually as bright as in new towns such as Columbia, every possibility of ecumenical planning to solve common building problems should always be pursued.

In addition, many churches are experimenting, some successfully, with weekday church-school and religious education during released time from the public schools. In other communities, imaginative programs are under way to broaden the impact of religious education on the community by a renewed concern for adult needs. Such concerns, which traditionally have been referred to committees on fellowship and recreation, have become part of the task of the Christian education committee.

Experiments in teaching techniques sometimes introduce new demands that must be considered by those charged with the planning of facilities. For example, many of the curricula of the larger denominations now include a strong emphasis on audio-visual aids; these require a room so arranged spatially that the most effective use can be made of the equipment. Many churches find that they use an audio-visual center in much the same way that colleges and public schools do. Teaching through closed-circuit TV will also become more common when the costs of installation and operation are reduced and when churches and denominations co-operate more closely in programs they cannot afford to undertake separately.

The appropriate committee must carefully review its entire Christian education program and ascertain whether some teaching might be more effective if conducted somewhere away from the church. This could be particularly pertinent in reaching adults. Perhaps the only way the church can provide adults with a significant program of Christian education is to take it to them—in their homes and in places convenient to their work, leisure, and recreation. In some communities the basement recreation room in a home may provide an atmosphere especially conducive to learning at some age levels. Similarly, the out-of-doors, community buildings, and other backgrounds might provide a better atmosphere for some learning experiences than classrooms erected on the church site. In particular, the use of community buildings might be an effective way to break down the atmosphere of exclusiveness associated with some churches.

CHAPTER ELEVEN

Places for Community Service

"The building . . . ought to be used to the limit to provide a place for the community to meet, to play, to learn, with no strings attached. The church, even in its architecture, is thus turned back into the world, opened out to it, for the sake of the world." [1]

—*George W. Webber*

The Protestant troika is worship, education, and fellowship—and a separate building is often provided for each. But can fellowship buildings be justified if their principal purpose is to provide for the leisure time of church members? George Webber argues that if the congregation is truly sensitive to the world about it, the buildings erected for fellowship and recreation will be available to the entire community as places for people to meet, play, and learn—"with no strings attached." He makes clear this does not mean that a church should ignore its own membership in providing for community needs, but he insists that concern for the needs of members is not enough. Webber is undoubtedly right. Concern for recreation and fellowship can be a temptation for a church to pamper itself with extravagant halls, stages, hobby rooms, and parlors, regardless of whether these can or will be used for community service.

Some of the difficulty in planning for community needs arises from our limited understanding of fellowship. To many, fellowship seems to mean nothing more than the sense of identification and companionship that can be developed through rummage sales, potluck suppers, and men's clubs—that is, miniature service clubs. The Greek word *koinonia* refers to the bond that ties disparate people together; more than activity, it is experienced by sharing a life of faith with others. And the kind of sharing that will nurture this relationship is most often found in serving others, including those who are not part of the group. To provide a place for this kind of relationship and service will result in a statement of program requirements that concentrates on the needs of the community the church should serve. It might be wise for the church *not* to name this facility a "fellowship hall." Calling it simply a "meeting hall" might better communicate the idea that the building is not exclusively for church members but is a place where all community groups could meet.

Existing Community Facilities Should Be Reviewed

A good way to begin preparing such a program is to inventory existing community facilities. Otherwise, churches will needlessly duplicate buildings that are readily available. For example, a few years ago many churches built gymnasiums more or less automatically, but today most of them are either musty, unused buildings, or have been remodeled to house other activities. This is an expensive way to discover that gymnasiums are normally provided in public schools or other community buildings. On the other hand, a Cleveland inner-city church, rebuilding in a blighted area, surveyed its parish and discovered that in the nearby area there were no public schools with gymnasiums. In this case, the building of a gymnasium was an opportunity to meet a community need.

As suggested in Chapter 2, needs should be defined in terms of persons as well as the various community organizations and social groups—for example, the needs of the teenager, the unmarried adult, the elderly, and those who are disadvantaged because of race or for any other reason. This does not mean, of course, that the church has a responsibility to provide facilities for every existing need. Its task will often consist of bringing sufficient political pressure to bear to make sure that government units will recognize their responsibilities. This will be especially true in communities that fail to provide needed facilities because of latent or open discrimination or *de facto* segregation. The church may also discover needs that might best be met through ecumenical planning and co-operation. If facilities are needed, two or more churches might erect buildings jointly at a substantial saving.

Practical Factors to Consider

A number of practical considerations must be faced in designing a place where people can gather for various activities. First, the room should not be too large. Just as it is a mistake to build a place of worship to accommodate the Easter crowd, so is it wrong to provide accommodations for occasional large gatherings. Provision should be made for adequate storage and for audio-visuals. The relationship of the facility to other buildings and to the parking area is important. The temptation to build a stage should be resisted; plays can be presented quite effectively in a room with portable platforms and portable lighting distribution and control centers. A large hotel-type kitchen is seldom needed, and, if a kitchenette will meet most requirements, nothing larger is needed; a caterer is far more economical and practical for those occasions which cannot be serviced otherwise.

If the committee concerned with Christian education has done a careful study, it will not overlook the need for a library. To be an effective educational tool, however, a library must first have the right books in it. This means a realistic budget to buy books, as no library should be forced to depend solely on donated books; these are frequently useless and often discourage those looking for an up-to-date discussion of a particular issue. The library should not be limited to what are often described as "spiritual books." Libraries so restricted often end up with books of only one type, mostly of mediocre quality. It is far better to adopt a broad policy, give basic responsibility to a selection committee, and trust readers to discriminate between books that have meaning for them and those that do not.

Location of the library is crucial. The church office is not usually satisfactory, but a room off the main corridor, where people regularly pass, would be ideal.

A Church Parlor?

Although intended to provide a place for people to meet informally, parlors are sometimes guilty of establishing an atmosphere of exclusiveness. Formal and forbidding, safely tucked away from the flow of traffic, they can easily suggest that they are to be "looked at" rather than "lived in," and are to be used only by the ingroup and their guests. On the other hand, a parlor can become the most used room in a church. Such a room should be easily accessible. For example, if it is to be used for serving coffee after worship services, it should be located near the narthex; otherwise, strangers will not easily find it. In addition, décor and furnishings should be inviting, clearly showing that the room is not simply a showpiece.

The parlor can serve many purposes. It ought to be a place where people can communicate easily with others and feel welcome and part of a group. Small groups might use it for meetings, along with some of the church organizations. It can also serve as a place for wedding receptions, anniversary observances, and other more formal events. The parlor could be used for art exhibitions and lectures, as well as a place where older youths would meet.

While some youth activities might take place in the parlor, many churches have found that the needs for a youth room are so disparate that it is necessary to provide a separate room for these meetings. Record players, soft drink dispensers, and the like are often desirable, but are usually not suitable in a parlor. If possible, however, the parlor should be co-ordinated with the youth room so that some common facilities can be planned, such as a kitchenette and storage rooms.

Facilities for Administration

Places for administration are obviously required to enable the staff to plan and carry out its assignments and responsibilities in an efficient and effective manner. While critics have decried the importance some churches apparently attach to administration, the results of poor organization are, inevitably, squandered opportunities and wasted resources. The dangers lie with churches and ministers that either ignore the importance of administration and thus do not function effectively as organizations, or allow organization to become an end in itself, to the detriment of mission.

Administrative facilities provide for a host of services, such as communication, co-ordination, staff offices, etc. When a new building is planned, one committee should devote substantial time to a study of administrative responsibilities, and specify what facilities will be needed. This will require an examination of the interrelationships among the various programs sponsored by the church, the relative responsibilities of the staff, the needs of the ministers and staff for places to study, work, and counsel, and the requirements for such items as mimeographing, mailing, and record-keeping. A written report should be developed, containing sufficient detail so the architect will be able to design the type of facilities needed.

But this housekeeping study is not the most important task of the committee. Administrative facilities are often the place where people contact the church on a most intimate and personal level. It is the place where the minister will counsel with those who are undergoing personal trials and difficulties, hold discussions with people who are considering membership in the church, or hold guidance sessions for young couples preparing for marriage.

To meet these requirements sensitively, the minister's study needs to be carefully designed, with the hope of accommodating a variety of needs. It should be located in a place that is easily and quickly accessible. To some, anonymity is important, and therefore it will be a great advantage if people can come and go with a minimum of contact with other members of the office staff or the public. The furnishings and décor of the study should be warm and friendly, functional and not pretentious. Proper planning of the study will make clear to the visitor that the minister is there to meet human needs, not to impress anyone with his power and importance.

One of the remarkable characteristics of the Christian faith is its unfolding nature, which offers to each generation the opportunity to find new insights in its ancient truths. Our generation has not failed to do this. The claim of the Gospel has increasingly become more clear. It is simply this: Today the church, if it is indeed to be the Church, must truly assume the stance of the servant. Many cannot believe this is possible so long as we continue to erect massive and extravagant church buildings that appear to be pathetic attempts at self-immortalization.

It is somewhat paradoxical that an age of affluence should be driven to question the integrity of monumental and self-seeking religious buildings, but perhaps this very affluence has made us more sensitive to the fact that we are a nation with thirty million deprived persons to whom the luxuries of a modern church building are unknown. The question seems to be: Can we continue to build churches at all when the specter of world-wide destitution can never be far from our consciences?

It is not enough to quote Jesus' words approving the extravagance of Magdalene, and to argue piously that nothing is too good for the house of God. We can no longer presume that God is impressed by our marble and brick, but must consider the likelihood that such buildings satisfy our own vanity and are often dedicated chiefly to our own ends.

But as we noted in the beginning, it is not an answer to say that men shall not build. By his very nature man is compelled to express his creativity and aspirations in the architecture of his environment. In fact, this is altogether fitting and proper for a creature made in God's image. As we face up to critical examination, therefore, the question becomes: What are we building a church for? To create a *tour de force* for our own pleasure? Hardly. For worship and education? Yes, of course. But is the building an appropriate place for service? Not superficial service, but the kind of Christian service that is appropriate for people who claim to follow the man of Nazareth.

This—the servant church—is the Church incarnate for our day.

Notes to Text

PART I: BUILDING WITH UNDERSTANDING

CHAPTER 1: TO BUILD A CHURCH

1. J. G. Davies, *The Secular Use of Church Buildings* (New York: The Seabury Press, 1968), p. 206.
2. Lyle E. Schaller, *Planning for Protestantism in Urban America* (New York and Nashville: Abingdon Press, 1965), pp. 123–127.
3. "This Architecture the Church Needs," an address delivered to the National Conference on Church Architecture, Cleveland, March, 20–22, 1962. Journal of the Conference, p. 13.
4. G. E. Kidder Smith, *The New Churches of Europe* (New York: Holt, Rinehart and Winston, 1964), pp. 13–14.
5. Quoted from an address entitled "Building for the Christian Parish in a Secular Culture," the National Conference on Church Architecture, Seattle, Wash., March 6, 1963. Journal of the Conference, p. 12.

CHAPTER 2: CHURCHES IN THE MIDST OF CHANGE

1. Quoted from an address to the International Congress on Religion, Architecture and the Visual Arts, New York City, August 28, 1967.
2. Quoted from an address by Paul Tillich, entitled "Honesty and Consecration in Religious Art and Architecture," the National Conference on Church Architecture, Chicago, Ill., April 29, 1965. Journal of the Conference, p. 74.
3. Dietrich Bonhoeffer, *Letters and Papers from Prison* (New York: Macmillan paperback, 1962), p. 162.
4. In an address to the International Congress on Religion, Architecture and the Visual Arts, New York City, August 28, 1967.
5. Tillich, *op. cit.,* fn. 2, p. 76.

CHAPTER 3: BUILDINGS THAT REFLECTED BELIEF— AND SOME THAT DID NOT

1. Journal of the National Conference on Church Architecture, Chicago, April 27–29, 1965, p. 22. Mr. Doom is Director of the Department

of Church Architecture, Board of Church Extension, Presbyterian Church in the United States.

2. In the 1630s Archbishop Laud had brought about a return of the altar/table to its medieval position against the wall of the chancel and had also succeeded in enclosing the altar/tables with rails at which communicants knelt to receive communion. The actions of the Long Parliament in 1640 temporarily put a stop to this custom, but, with the Restoration in 1660, Laudian tradition was revived, and most, but not all, churches built during the Wren period provided altars erected against the wall that were also set apart by railings. G. W. O. Addleshaw and Frederick Etchells, *The Architectural Setting of Anglican Worship* (London: Faber and Faber Ltd., 1948), pp. 120 ff.

3. James F. White, *Protestant Worship and Church Architecture* (New York: Oxford University Press, 1964), p. 107.

CHAPTER 4: OF ART AND SYMBOLS

1. Mr. Maguire is an architect and author. This quotation appears in an essay entitled "Meaning and Understanding," in *Towards a Church Architecture,* Peter Hammond, ed. (London: The Architectural Press, 1962), p. 66.

2. Albert Christ-Janer and Mary Mix Foley, *Modern Church Architecture* (New York: McGraw-Hill, 1962), p. 122.

3. Quoted from an address to the International Congress on Religion, Architecture and the Visual Arts, New York City, August 30, 1967.

4. *Ibid.*

5. Selden Rodman, *Conversations with Artists* (New York: Devin-Adair, 1957), pp. 93–94.

PART II: ARCHITECT, BUILDING COMMITTEE, SITE, AND MASTER PLAN: CRITICAL CONCERNS FOR THE BUILDING ENTERPRISE

CHAPTER 5: A KEY PERSON: THE ARCHITECT

1. Quoted from an address to the International Congress on Religion, Architecture and the Visual Arts, New York City, August 30, 1967.

CHAPTER 6: THE WRITTEN PROGRAM

1. Edward S. Frey, *This Before Architecture* (Jenkintown, Pa.: Religious Publishing Co., 1963), p. 108. Dr. Frey is Executive Director, Commission on Church Architecture, Lutheran Church in America.

2. See pages 170–171 for addresses of many denominational building consultants.
3. 475 Riverside Drive, New York, N.Y. 10027.

CHAPTER 7: SELECTING THE SITE

1. Quoted from an address delivered to the International Congress on Religion, Architecture and the Visual Arts, New York City, August 31, 1967.
2. Lyle E. Schaller, *Planning for Protestantism in Urban America*, pp. 98–112.

CHAPTER 8: THE MASTER PLAN

1. As quoted by Philip Deane, *Constantinos Doxiadis, Master Builder for Free Men* (Dobbs Ferry, N.Y.: Oceana Publications, 1965), p. 15.

PART III: FORM, FUNCTION, AND BELIEF

CHAPTER 9: PLACES FOR WORSHIP

1. As quoted in *The New York Times*, August 28, 1965, p. 18.
2. James F. White, *Protestant Worship and Church Architecture*, Chapter I.
3. Liturgical Conference (ed.), *Priest's Guide to Parish Worship* (Baltimore: Garamond/Pridemark Press, 1964), pp. 26, 115.
4. Donald J. Bruggink and Carl H. Droppers, *Christ and Architecture* (Grand Rapids, Mich.: William B. Eerdmans Publishing Co., 1965), p. 211.
5. J. G. Davies, *Worship and Mission* (London: SCM Press Ltd., 1966), p. 19.
6. ———. *The Secular Use of Church Buildings*, pp. 238–239.
7. Quoted from an address entitled "New Visions for Church Builders," delivered at the National Conference on Church Architecture, Pittsburgh, Pa., April 19, 1961. Journal of the Conference, pp. 18–19.
8. "The Shape of Our Places of Worship," in *Protestant Church Buildings and Equipment*, May 1960.
9. Peter Hammond (ed.), *Towards a Church Architecture* (London: The Architectural Press, 1962), p. 27. "An altar over twenty feet long seems to call for a celebrant thirteen or fourteen feet high: and for all its alleged comprehensiveness it may reasonably be doubted whether the Church of England is equal to meeting such a demand."
10. James A. Whyte, "A Place for the Preaching of the Word," in *Churchbuilding*, April 1963.

11. Howard G. Hageman, *Pulpit and Table* (Richmond, Va.: John Knox Press, 1962), p. 112.
12. See Gilbert Cope, *Symbolism in the Bible and the Church* (New York: Philosophical Library), p. 104.

CHAPTER 10: SPACE, FORM, AND CHRISTIAN EDUCATION

1. Lyle E. Schaller, *Planning for Protestantism in Urban America* (New York and Nashville: Abingdon Press, 1965), p. 205.
2. Roger L. Shinn, *The Educational Mission of Our Church* (Boston and Philadelphia: United Church Press, 1962), p. 20.
3. Mildred C. Widber and Scott Turner Ritenour, *Focus: Building for Christian Education* (Boston and Philadelphia: Pilgrim Press, 1969). Published for Cooperative Publishers Association.

CHAPTER 11: PLACES FOR COMMUNITY SERVICE

1. George W. Webber, *The Congregation in Mission* (New York and Nashville: Abingdon Press, 1964), p. 177.

—••≪ ❊ ≫••—

Appendices

I: HOW TO CONDUCT A BUILDING NEEDS STUDY *
(To be used particularly in conjunction with Chapter 6)

A building program requires careful preparation from its inception. A church's approach to planning can be decisive. The method is much the same, whether the church is large or small, whether it is the first unit for a new church or an education building for an established church. But the results will be different for each church, since no two are alike and there are no stock solutions for building problems. There are recommended procedures for any congregation launching building programs, but each must determine what type of building will best meet its needs.

As soon as the congregation has agreed that a building program is needed, the time has come for study and organization, putting first things first. Unfortunately, some congregations, once they decide to build, rush out to employ an architect to prepare designs and plans.

The first step in the development of a program is an evaluation of immediate needs and a look into the future—five, ten, or even twenty years. The church as a whole must develop this program—not the architect, the pastor, a board of trustees, or a small group of members. The program should indicate the church's reason for being, its theology, its purposes; it can come only from the study and involvement of the entire congregation.

Such a study is not only exciting in itself but can bring out hidden talents, educate members regarding the life of the church, and deepen the commitment of participants. It can even be a significant means of evangelism in the community.

A well-guided program results in a written document that includes discussion of these major questions:

1. What is the true meaning of the church?
2. What are the beliefs, the theology, and the guiding principles that are relevant to carrying out its tasks and meeting its responsibilities?

* Adapted from *Planning to Build* by John E. Morse and August Burchardt, published by United Church Board for Homeland Ministries. (Used by permission.)

3. Why is the church in this community? What is its mission, its purpose, its tasks?

4. What is the history of the church and what are its future responsibilities? How can it meet these challenges and opportunities?

The church that can answer these questions with perception and insight has begun to know itself; it will also have taken the first basic steps toward good architecture. Using this platform, the architect can design a building that will interpret the program, belief, and theology of the church.

ORGANIZING THE COMMITTEES

Study and planning require careful organization. Study committees may be appointed by the chairman of the official board or the church president, or they may be elected by the congregation on recommendation of the nominating committee. The minister and the officers of the church should assume responsibility for co-ordinating the work of the program committees to assure that their tasks are being performed effectively and efficiently. Experience has shown that it is best to designate a chairman for each study committee at the time of appointment or election.

The following committees are recommended:

1. Survey
2. Worship
3. Christian Education
4. Service
5. Administrative Facilities
6. Publicity
7. Finance
8. Furnishings and Equipment
9. Executive Building Committee

The first five are program committees whose major responsibilities are discharged with the preparation of the written program. The last four are working committees, which serve during the entire study and building period and have special responsibilities. The Executive Building Committee implements the work of all the committees. This does not mean that the working committees have nothing to do while the program committees are at work; each has its contribution to make toward the completion of a written report of committee findings and recommendations.

The Executive Building Committee is elected or appointed to implement the building program after the written program is completed. Small churches may find it necessary to reduce the number of committees to Survey, Worship, Finance, Publicity, Education and Service, and the Executive Building Committee.

If possible, the Executive Building Committee should include representatives from the various study committees. Its task is to review all committee work, interview and recommend an architect, and, in general, see that the building is designed and erected in accordance with the program and financial ability of the church.

In churches with a membership of less than 150, every member—both men and women—should be asked to serve on a committee; in larger churches, at least one member of each family. Some will not accept, others will not serve effectively, but the general availability of this opportunity is a unifying force. The president or moderator of the church will be an ex officio member of each committee.

Two pitfalls to be avoided are: having a church board constitute itself a committee, and having too many people with similar backgrounds on the same committee. For example, besides schoolteachers and those with allied interests, others could make a contribution to the Christian Education Committee. A balanced committee membership will result in a truly representative program rather than one restricted to the interests of various ingroups.

Even grumblers should be included; sometimes they turn out to be people waiting to be guided into constructive activity by diplomatic leadership. If their talents are tested by the committee process, they often become more co-operative, and there is always the possibility that one of their "peculiar" ideas is exactly right in a particular situation.

It is important to explain to each committee the nature of its task and responsibility. Members should be provided with resource material, and, of course, the value of the committee system is lost unless opportunity is given for full discussion and explanation. (See Bibliography for recommended sources.)

SURVEY COMMITTEE

(This committee will be most concerned with the material in Chapters 1–3, 6, and 7.)

The task of the Survey Committee is to gather statistical and other information in order to provide basic data upon which the church can estimate its immediate and future needs. Its first task is to define the parish. In the case of new churches, this is often done by comity agreements in a state or local council of churches; sometimes the parish may be city-wide, as in a downtown church situation. Where comity does not exist, a new church may select the area it might reasonably serve. A line drawn around this area may be square, circular, oval, or irregular, depending on the particular situation. If comity approval has not been obtained, the project should, wherever possible, be cleared through the comity committee of the local council of churches.

A church will want to take a census, sometimes called a "religious census," of this area. The information obtained should be as detailed as possible, including the number of people in the area, their approximate ages, whether they own their homes, their occupations, and so forth. The census will provide guidelines for the church in evaluating its program and as a basis for estimating future needs. For example, the census will show the percentage of population in the major faiths—that is, Protestant, Roman Catholic, Jewish—and also the number of persons not affiliated with a church. The average age of the residents of the parish and the number of children will be of great importance to the educational committee and those planning for recreational needs. Projected growth statistics are vital to the work of all the committees.

Survey members should make contact with leaders in the local schools and hold conferences with them on their plans for the years ahead. Obviously, the location and size of public schools are significant data. Estimates of growth potential can be secured from utility companies, along with any plans for expansion that may affect the parish. The likelihood of industrial growth and other developments affecting population also need to be taken into consideration. Information should be gathered from zoning agencies, county and city planning commissions, and, in the case of churches with rural membership, government farm agencies in the area. The population and number of homes in the area can be determined from the census and other sources; the next step is to evaluate turnover in population. Age groupings in the parish should be estimated; therefore it would be advisable to prepare a large spot map showing the residences of the present membership and those of potential future members. With this information in hand, a reasonable effort at projecting statistics can be made.

The facts gathered by the survey committee should be put into writing and given to the other committees and to the Executive Building Committee. Many important decisions will depend on how careful a job it has done in gathering statistics and analyzing their importance.

WORSHIP COMMITTEE

(This committee will be most concerned with the contents of Chapters 1–6, 8, and 9.)

This group could well be called a committee on the theology of worship, as one of its principal functions is to examine the beliefs of the church as related to its worship practices. What a church believes determines to a great degree the way in which the church worships, and the way a church worships has a significant part to play in planning a church building. Thus it is the responsibility of this committee to examine carefully the church's theology of worship and to express it in writing, insofar as this is possible.

This committee must necessarily take on an extensive amount of reading and research. Close counsel and leadership from the pastor are imperative as it grapples with such questions as: What does the congregation believe about Baptism and Communion? What is the purpose of the liturgy? What is the meaning of the chancel? What is symbolism and the purpose of symbolism? Should the church have a pulpit only or a pulpit and a lectern? What is the meaning of an altar, a communion table? Should a communion table be used as an altar and should a communion table be removed from the back wall of the chancel? Is the same true of an altar? Where should the choir sit? What is the place of music in the liturgy? Is the choir to be located in the chancel and sing to the congregation, or is the choir to be a worshiping choir, perhaps sitting in the balcony or other area facing the chancel as they sing, somewhat as the worshipers do? Where should the baptismal font be located? Why?

Another important aspect of this committee's work is the study and evaluation of the use of art in the church building, especially as related to worship. The church was once the principal source and inspiration for many of the great works of art, but in modern times this opportunity and responsibility have been widely neglected. As a result, the art found in church buildings is often poor in concept and in execution, and sometimes at serious odds with the church's teaching.

Because of the complexities in this field, the committee may find it advisable to divide itself into subcommittees to study music and choir, liturgy, art and symbolism, and so forth.

The average worshiper often does not understand the purpose of a worship service. The Worship Committee has an opportunity to communicate with the church members on the meaning, significance, and methods of Christian worship. Its findings will have an important bearing on the architecture of the buildings to be erected, whether they are designed as education buildings or as worship units.

CHRISTIAN EDUCATION COMMITTEE

(This committee will be most concerned with the contents of Chapters 1–6, 8 and 10; it will also need several copies of *Focus: Building for Christian Education*. See Bibliography.)

The scope of the Christian Education Committee is broader than is generally realized. Its responsibility not only includes the traditional Sunday morning church school but also the educational needs in the many related programs of the church, including evening youth groups, special facilities for adults, day nurseries, daytime programs for the elderly and others. The committee will more easily keep in mind all these areas of responsibility if its membership is not composed solely of church school-teachers. The minister, the director of religious education, and/or the superintendent of the church school, and representatives from the official board or committee of the church responsible for Christian education would obviously be useful on it. There is also a need for people who are not specifically connected with the church school but whose general experience, curiosity, and willingness to learn will encourage a re-examination of philosophy and purpose, as well as technique and method.

The Education Committee should get in touch with its denominational offices concerned with Christian education to obtain literature and information. Members should attend any special conferences in the area on church building or religious education. Visits to neighboring church-school facilities may well be useful. Again, the goal of the over-all committee will be a written program. Because of heavy responsibilities, appointment of subcommittees to deal with the various age groupings and educational programs of the church is often helpful.

COMMITTEE ON SERVICE

(This committee will be most concerned with the contents of Chapters 1–6, 8, and 11.)

The task of the Committee on Service is to define the program of the church in terms of service. This is the place for such concerns as the needs of community and the congregation and their space requirements. The committee should also examine the possibility for multiuse of existing buildings, as well as make an inventory of existing community facilities to see if additional construction is actually required.

The committee also has the task of evaluating traditional church fellowship programs and suggesting which of these programs should be carried forward into the new buildings. Erecting a new building is often a good time to terminate programs that have outlived their usefulness.

The findings of other committees should be studied to determine whether their functions overlap. Care must be exercised to meet the requirements of all needed programs, but the committee should be careful that its requests for space are realistic in terms of anticipated use.

ADMINISTRATIVE FACILITIES COMMITTEE

(This committee will be most concerned with the contents of Chapters 1–6, 8, and 11.)

The word "administration" often summons up a picture of desks, typewriters, janitor supplies, and other housekeeping needs of the church. While these cannot be overlooked, the job of the Administrative Facilities Committee is much broader. It must first come to an understanding of the administrative responsibility of the pastor and appreciate its importance. In addition to his many pastoral responsibilities, the pastor is often the principal contact between the church and the public. Day-to-day concerns of the church institution and its program usually find their way to his desk, and many people make their first tentative contacts with the church through administrative facilities, frequently in a counseling relationship with the minister. Whether the minister has facilities to write, to study, and to prepare himself for Sunday services depends principally on the work of this committee, as does the work space allocated for secretarial help.

This committee should also address itself to such questions as outdoor facilities and parking needs. By co-ordinating its work with other committees, particularly the committee on Service and the Christian Education Committee, it will make certain that such needs as libraries, bridal rooms, reception and conference rooms, and rooms for staff workers are considered. The needs of part-time employees of the church, such as a place for the caretaker to keep his tools and equipment, must not be forgotten.

Again, the objective is a written program to submit to the Executive Building Committee for its use and study.

PUBLICITY COMMITTEE

Publicity links the church and the community. The more the community and the membership know about the church's program, the more likely it is that the church will find itself in a position of community leadership.

Among its more obvious duties, this committee should become acquainted with the church editor of the local newspaper, keeping him supplied with information for possible stories concerning the present and developing program of the church. News directors of local radio and television stations are also important contacts. Another aspect of Publicity's job is to make sure that all study committees place news items in the local church bulletin or monthly newsletter, and in the area paper published by the denominational or other office. The work of the study committees also needs to be publicized effectively within the membership. Publicity pictures, taken at regular intervals, will provide visual reporting of the committees' operations, the site of the new building, building progress, and, of course, its completion. A carefully used placard may be highly effective, particularly if made by the church school in co-operation with the Christian Education Committee.

FINANCE COMMITTEE

(The recommendations found in Appendix IV, Financing the Building Program, will be of concern to this committee.)

No matter how noble and intelligent the plans for a church building program may be, a church can build only what it can finance.

The average person, knowing what he can afford on his own income, too often looks at a church debt as if it were all his own to pay, forgetting the ability inherent in a committed church fellowship. It is the responsibility of the Finance Committee to see that the full potential of the committed group is realized, without overextension; it needs to ascertain as nearly as possible the average income of the membership, the economic base of the community, and other statistics that have a bearing on the financial ability of the congregation.

A conference should be arranged with denominational executives and, if possible, with church building consultants serving the denomination to obtain guidance and information on ways and means to finance the building program. Properly planned capital funds campaigns are usually necessary and desirable; in such campaigns timing is all important. Not only will these campaigns provide financial undergirding, but they may stimulate evangelism and over-all stewardship of time and talents. Many churches state that the by-products of the campaign are even more important than the financial results. There is a search for the total meaning of stewardship, not just for the building program but for current and benevolent funds as well.

Since nearly every church has to borrow funds for building, the committee may wish to visit local lending institutions from time to time and keep them posted on developments. The committee need not ask for a loan, but can prepare the lender for a possible approach, giving him a clear understanding of the needs and abilities of the group.

Whether the loan funds come from a local lending institution or from denominational resources, the amount that can be obtained usually depends on the ability to repay. The monthly income pledged to the building fund will be weighed by the lender against the amount of the loan, the term and interest rate, and the general health of the church program as he understands it. For every $1,000 monthly payment of principal and interest, there should be at least $1,100 in monthly pledges to cover the payments. Experience indicates that a church should allow for a 10 percent shrinkage, as not every pledge will be paid. Some members will move away, others will lose interest or simply be unable to meet their pledges. The work sheet for building-debt analysis at the conclusion of this section should be studied and completed by this committee to guide the church in analyzing its financial capability.

The work of the Finance Committee should continue as a subcommittee of the Executive Building Committee until the financing of the new building is completely arranged. While not a program study committee in the same sense as the others, it is important that the Finance Committee put its findings in writing and report to the congregation at regular intervals. Like all committees, it should work closely with the Publicity Committee.

FURNISHINGS AND EQUIPMENT COMMITTEE

The membership of this committee should include representatives from the Worship, Christian Education, Service, and Administrative Facilities committees, together with such other persons as the church may consider desirable to appoint or elect. It need not be organized until after the other committees are set up, since its principal work will not begin until the program study committees have tentative recommendations regarding equipment and furnishing needs; it should continue to function during construction under the direction of the Executive Building Committee.

Since this committee must prepare a complete check list of all furniture and equipment to be installed in that portion or portions of the building complex to be constructed, its first step is to study these needs as defined in the written reports of the other committees. Furniture and equipment owned by the church must be evaluated to determine what items can be used in the new facility. A master list of needed furnishings and equipment, with notations as to usable existing furnishings, should then be prepared for the Executive Building Committee. (Mechanical equipment normally remains the responsibility of the architect and the Executive Building Committee.)

The architect will be able to suggest sources of supply, prices and samples of all furnishings and equipment, and should be asked to serve as a consultant to this committee. Without his services, furnishings may be chosen that are not harmonious in color and design or are not appropriate to the function of the building. Frequently, the architect can design items to be custom-built with good results; his fee for these additional services is usually nominal, and the resulting co-ordinated furnishings are usually worth the extra cost.

Since members of this committee will have served on one or another of the major program study committees, there is general familiarity with the basic source materials. One can only repeat those suggestions described in the sections discussing the study committee responsibilities.

EXECUTIVE BUILDING COMMITTEE

The Executive Building Committee is a working committee and its duties continue long after the program is written; its responsibility is to implement the findings of the study committees. It recommends an architect and works closely with him and others outside the congregation in the development of the building design. Together with the Finance Committee, it will develop final details of financing the construction; along with the Furnishings and Equipment Committee, it will provide answers to the church's needs for these items. It should be familiar with all the material in this book.

Membership should include representatives from each program study committee and from the Furnishings and Equipment, Publicity, and Finance committees. The time for appointments or election is after other committees have finished their studies and the written program is completed and approved. Knowledge of a building trade is not necessary. A word of caution: No one should be placed on this committee who could have a vested interest. An architect, contractor, decorator, organist, or engineer might be influenced by his professional bias and not see the program as a whole.

The committee's responsibility is a broad one. It will:

1. Send the written program of the church to the denominational church building consultant for comment.

2. Establish preliminary contact with leadership for a capital funds program.

3. Find and recommend the architect, following approved procedures. (Note the recommendations in Chapter 5 for selecting the architect at an earlier time under some circumstances.)

4. See that the architect chosen is supplied with complete information, including a copy of the written building program.

5. Take necessary steps to clear title to the site.

6. Request the architect to prepare a master plan, i.e., an over-all schematic plot plan of the ultimate building development on the site.

7. Send master plan and preliminary drawings to the denominational church building consultant for review and comment.

8. After approval of master plan and preliminary drawings by the church and the denominational church building department, if there is one, obtain estimates of cost from the architect and contractors.

9. Review financial situation with Finance Committee and act on its recommendations.

10. Secure working drawings and specifications for those portions the church plans to construct at the present time.

11. Investigate and recommend a list of suitable contractors who will be asked to bid. There is no point in including anyone on the list to whom the committee would be uneasy awarding the contract if his bid turned out to be the low one.

12. Award contracts. Follow carefully the counsel of the architect, who now becomes the business agent.

13. Provide for landscaping of the new facilities, and co-operate with the Furnishings and Equipment Committee in providing for adequate furnishings.

14. Appoint a small subcommittee of two or three persons to act as sole contact between the contractor, Executive Building Committee, and architect in order to avoid conflicting instructions, overlapping, and confusion. These persons need not be members of the Executive Building Committee; they can be called a "plans and construction" subcommittee.

15. Continue as a responsible committee until the construction is completed.

SUGGESTED METHODS FOR COMMITTEE OPERATION

Committees should meet separately twice a month, if possible, giving adequate opportunity for information and material to be presented, evaluated, and discussed; tentative conclusions should be put into writing. At each meeting previous conclusions may need to be reviewed and revised in the light of new information developed by the committee.

After approximately three months of study, the official board, minister, or officers of the church should co-ordinate the preparation of preliminary mimeographed statements of conclusions reached by the committees to be circulated to the congregation and later presented at a meeting of the entire membership. Friends of the church ought to be encouraged to participate in the meeting—a dinner meeting, planned for fellowship, is perhaps the best solution. At this time the chairman of each committee should briefly present the tentative findings of his committee and solicit questions and comments. It is better to have disagreements and misunderstandings arise at this point, while resolution is possible, rather than after a building has been completed.

There will be need for most committees to continue their work of gathering and evaluating information at regular meetings. After another three months, a congregational meeting should be held to bring the members and friends up to date on the progress of the study committees. When the study committees have completed their work, a congregational meeting is again held to discuss, approve, and revise the proposed study committee reports. This seems the appropriate point at which to elect or appoint the Executive Building Committee. When the congregation has given its approval to the work of the study committees, the church has a written, documented program.

Such a program, obviously, cannot be prepared overnight. A number of months must elapse. Much depends upon the determination and diligence of the members. If too much time is taken, the group may hit a plateau and become listless, but a rushed atmosphere can result in an abortive study. The average time is from ten to fourteen months. Many find this to be a short period, because of the complexities of the task and the deepening of interest and concern.

SUGGESTED ORDER OF PROCEDURE

(Note: If the denominational church building department recommends a different timetable, such recommendations should be followed.)

1. Study committees prepare written documented program.
2. Congregation approves program. Executive Building Committee is elected or appointed.
3. Program is submitted to denominational church building consultant.
4. Congregation approves capital funds project and authorizes signing of contract for services of a qualified leader.
5. Executive Building Committee interviews and recommends architect and submits qualifications with proposed contract to denominational church building consultant. (Note the recommendations in Chapter 5 on selecting the architect at an earlier time under certain circumstances.)
6. Architect is approved by congregation at congregational meeting.
7. Executive Building Committee and Finance Committee review and define financial ability.
8. Architect submits master plan and preliminary drawings of first unit to be built.
9. Executive Building Committee approves preliminary plans and master plan and submits them to denominational church building consultant.
10. Congregational meeting:
    a. Approves master plan and preliminary drawings of first unit.
    b. Reviews financing.
11. Church conducts capital funds campaign.
12. Executive Building Committee makes tentative financing arrangements.
13. Congregational meeting:
    a. Gives final approval of preliminary drawings.
    b. Approves financing arrangements.

WORK SHEET FOR BUILDING DEBT ANALYSIS

CHURCH:_____

A. BUILDING REQUIREMENTS:

1. Contract
   (estimate)(actual) $_____
2. Contingencies
   (10% of contract)   _____
3. Utility connections
   and site development _____
4. Architect's fees   _____
5. Furnishings (est.)   _____
6. Cost of site   _____
7. Other   _____
   Total $_____

Existing capital
   indebtedness on:

Church buildings $_____

Parsonage $_____

Site $_____

Other $_____

B. PLANS TO FINANCE:

1. Cash on hand $_____
2. Pledges payable
   prior to completion   _____
3. Mortgage
   financing from

   _____

   for _____years
   at_____% interest   _____
4. Other sources for
   financing   _____

   Total $_____

Note:

The total of Plans to Finance (Sec. B) should balance with Building Requirements (Sec. A). The total of Monthly Income (Sec. C) should balance with Monthly Payments (Sec. D).

C. INCOME FROM BUILDING PLEDGES:

Campaign directed by_____on_____resulted in
pledges of $_____ payable over_____years by_____
                                                      (date)

The Monthly Income from these pledges is estimated as follows:

Monthly building income pledged $_____
Less 10% shrinkage   _____
Estimated monthly pledge income $_____

D. CAPITAL INDEBTEDNESS:

The following debts are to be paid from income from building pledges:

Monthly payments of principal and interest,
   1st mortgage loan $_____
Monthly payments of principal and interest,
   2nd mortgage loan   _____
Other payments on debts   _____
   Total monthly payments $_____

14. Architect prepares and submits working drawings and specifications.
15. Congregational meeting:
    a. Approves working drawings.
    b. Instructs Executive Building Committee to obtain bids from contractors.
16. Congregational meeting:
    a. Executive Building Committee recommends contractor and bid.
    b. Congregational approval.
17. Executive Building Committee appoints small subcommittee to act as sole contact between it and the contractor and architect.
18. Groundbreaking.
19. Construction.
20. Dedication.

II: CRITICAL QUESTIONS IN SELECTING A CHURCH SITE
(Note: This section is to be used in conjunction with Chapter 7.)

CITY   STATE   DATE
CHURCH, OR DESIGNATION OF PROPOSED NEW CHURCH
LOCATION OF PROPOSED SITE

1. What is the approximate population of the area within a one-mile radius of the proposed site?
2. Is the population center shifting? If so, where will the future population center be?
3. Is the proposed site compatible with church planning or comity?
4. Has a religious census been taken? If so, what guidelines does this provide in selecting a site?
5. What type of homes (single-family, duplex, apartments, etc.) are in the area that the church will naturally serve?
6. Are new homes being constructed in the area? If so, what is the rate of construction?
7. Are residents in the area largely transients or long-term home owners?
8. Are there any social factors that would make the work of a church unusually difficult?
9. Are there any special needs of the community?
10. Has the Municipal or Country Planning Commission been consulted to determine future plans for the area?
11. Can the property be reached by public transportation? How?
12. Are public utilities (gas, electricity, telephone, water) available? If not available, what would the cost be to obtain needed utilities?
13. Will a church situated on this site primarily serve a neighborhood or a wider area?
14. Is the site near flight lanes of an airport, fire stations, heavy traffic routes, or other things that are likely to create a noise problem?

15. Are there underminings in the area? If so, does the title to the property reserve mineral rights to others?

16. Are there other soil conditions that might affect foundation requirements for large buildings erected on the site?

17. Have soil-test borings been made to ascertain whether normal footings will suffice?

18. Is the site adequately drained? Has the site ever been flooded? Are storm sewers installed or needed?

19. What are the dimensions of the site? Its frontage?

20. Is there enough usable land for a church complex with adequate provisions for off-street parking? (See question No. 35.)

21. What off-street parking is available within two blocks of the site?

22. What is the price? Are there special terms available?

23. Is the price a fair one when compared to nearby property values?

24. What is the topography compared to the surrounding area?

25. Will a church building be easily visible to passing travelers?

26. What percentage of the land within one and a half miles of the site is undeveloped? What are the plans for the future development of the area?

27. Is the land too low for a basement?

28. Is the site near any businesses that may be objectionable, such as filling stations, restaurants, stores, etc. that remain open on Sunday.

29. How far is the site from a major shopping area? Will people pass the site en route to downtown shopping areas?

30. Is the site on a corner? If so, is there a stop sign at the corner?

31. If the site is on a corner, is it safe for small children to cross the streets?

32. How far is the site from a public school? A parochial school? Where are the school-district boundaries in relation to the site?

33. Are there any offensive odors in the surrounding area?

34. Describe any natural barriers such as rivers, lakes, hills, ravines, etc., which may be nearby. Also state if site is adjacent or near to golf courses, parks, cemeteries, tourist courts, railroads, industrial areas, heavily traveled highways, large power lines, outdoor movies, pipelines, old barns, or run-down property.

35. Does city or county law require that buildings for public use have off-street parking? If so, what are these regulations and requirements?

36. Is site within a zoned area, and, if so, what are zoning requirements?

37. What are the legal requirements for setback of buildings on site?

38. Is proposed site encumbered by special assessments?

39. Will there be future assessments for streets, sewers, curbs, sidewalks, etc.? If so, what are estimated costs? Will the municipality require a new fire hydrant on the church site as a condition of building?

40. What restrictions or covenants are against the title of the property? Is there any restriction existing or proposed that would limit use of the site to church purposes only?

41. What easements exist on the property, and what are their locations?
42. If site is purchased, will seller provide title insurance, and at whose expense?
43. Has the property been surveyed in recent years? Does the survey disclose any boundary encroachments? Will the financing agent require a new survey, and, if so, what will the cost be? Will the seller bear the cost of survey?

III: HOW TO SELECT AN ARCHITECT
(Note: This appendix should be used in conjunction with Chapter 5.)

The committee responsible for engaging an architect should obtain the names of architects recommended by committee members, denominational sources (including denominational church building offices), and such sources as local councils of churches, the Commission on Church Building and Architecture of the National Council of Churches, and those recommended by such organizations as the Guild for Religious Architecture and the American Institute of Architects.* Membership in a professional society does not in itself guarantee quality of design, but the membership directory can point to architects who have an interest in church design and some experience in this field.

Committees need not restrict themselves to architects practicing in the immediate community. Transportation today is so easy and fast that architects can work with satisfactory results for churches some distance from their office. In dealing with an architect from another community, a committee will, of course, want to satisfy itself that the architect will do the necessary travel to maintain contact with the committee and oversee the construction.

Early in the process, the committee should narrow the list of names by reviewing dossiers and making preliminary inquiries to ascertain whether particular architects are interested in being considered. If possible, the list of likely candidates should be narrowed to not more than five—preferably to three or four.

The committee can then proceed to arrange interviews with the architects under consideration. In fairness to the architect, ample time should be allowed. For example, two interviews should not be scheduled for the same evening, with the resulting pressure to finish the first interview by a certain time.

In preparing for the interview, committee members should become familiar with what an architect does and how he goes about it. They ought to know something about the fee arrangements recommended in the AIA

---

* Churches interested in studying the professional standards of the American Institute of Architects can write to the institute at 1735 New York Ave., N.W., Washington, D.C. 20036, or obtain copies from local Institute chapters or from architects who are members of the Institute.

standard form of contract, and be prepared to ask questions that will develop the information they need to reach a decision. Such considerations include:

1. What is the architect's philosophy of church design?

2. What questions does the architect have concerning the program and special problems of the church? A good architect must be able to make a clear analysis of the architectural problem, and separate the real needs of the church from arbitrary or unrealistic preferences. The manner in which the architect probes and the questions he asks are excellent clues to his ability and interest.

3. Will the architect be willing to make schematic studies until they are approved by the church?

4. Will the architect design some of the furnishings, such as pews and chancel appointments, and advise in the selection of other furnishings? What will the fee be for these services? A skilled co-ordination of furnishings is necessary for proper functioning as well as for the aesthetics of a good building.

5. The architect should be asked to explain his fee fully and provide a copy of the proposed fee contract for the committee to study. Related questions are: Does the fee include the preparation of a model? If not, and a model is desired, what will the extra cost be? Does the fee include an over-all master plan for the site development, and what does the architect understand a "master plan" to be? Will the congregation be obligated to employ the architect for any future building done in accordance with the master plan? What will the respective rights and liabilities of the parties be if the project is abandoned at various stages, that is, before preliminary drawings, after preliminaries, after working drawings? What will the respective responsibilities be if the lowest bid exceeds the architect's cost estimate? What procedure does the architect follow in preparing a cost estimate?

6. How does the architect present a proposed preliminary plan to the congregation for approval?

7. How does the architect supervise construction? Who in the architect's office actually does the supervising?

8. Would the volume of work to which the architect is already committed prevent him from meeting the church's required timetable? How much time is estimated between approval of preliminary drawings and completion of working drawings and specifications?

Upon the committee's reaching a decision as to the architect it wishes to recommend, employment of the architect ought to be cleared through any denominational offices whose approval is required. After this, one name should be recommended to the congregation or official board of the church for approval.

EVALUATING THE ARCHITECT

The committee should first look at the architect's background and training—that is, the committee would be well advised to insist that all architects considered have an excellent history of education and experience.

Suggested areas of inquiry are:

What schools did the architect attend? With what firms has he been associated? To what professional associations does he belong? Is he a member of the American Institute of Architects? It is also wise to find out whether the architect is affiliated with organizations especially concerned with church architecture.

Does he understand the vital concerns of a church? This does not mean that he must be an active church member, but it is necessary that the architect understand, appreciate, and be sensitive to the needs and program of a church.

Also—what of his ability as a designer? This is extremely hard to judge. The committee should examine examples of his work, but these need not necessarily be confined to church buildings. It is foolish, however, to criticize the architect or rule him out merely because the design of a particular building does not conform to the committee's concept of what it should be. Every building should be evaluated solely in terms of whether it expresses the needs, wishes, and personality of the owner, not that of some other person.

References from former clients are important. Inquiry should be made as to how the architect worked with committees involved in the planning of the building. What is his personality, especially in group relationships? Did he use reasonable care in looking after his clients' interests? Did he show adequate knowledge of the needs and functions of a church? How did his cost estimates compare with the bids? Did his office act responsibly in supervising the construction? How has the building served functionally? What has the experience in maintenance costs been? If problems exist in maintenance or function, are they the result of misjudgment by the architect or failure of the client to specify his program accurately?

The question may arise as to whether a committee should consider an architect who has never designed a church. To rule out such men automatically would write off some of our finest architects. Past experience in designing churches should be considered, but, regardless of experience, the essential question remains: Can an architect translate sympathetically and with integrity the needs and theology of a church into form and space? The architect who has this ability can design a great church building, whether or not it is his first one.

Technical knowledge, of course, is important. While an architect may not also be an engineer, a good architect will have as associates men who can provide the necessary technical skills. Again, client references can provide a basis for evaluation of the architect's over-all performance.

It is easier to describe the architect a church should *not* employ. If an architect is always agreeable to any suggestions, if he is simply a "yes man," he will do a church a disservice. There are times when a conscientious architect must say "no" to his client to maintain the integrity of his own convictions. On the other hand, a good architect is not arbitrary and self-righteous, but is always seeking to reach areas of common understanding.

Committees should avoid an architect whose work, even though he has built many churches, seems stale and stereotyped rather than creative and fresh. Such an architect may simply be repeating past mistakes, while representing himself as an expert in church building. By the same token, the architect for whom each commission is merely another opportunity for experimentation, with little regard for the needs of the client, should also be avoided.

The architect who offers a cut-rate deal is subject to serious question. A church should expect to pay a normal fee consistent with that charged by competent architects in the community.

The qualifications of an architect who habitually misses the mark on his cost estimates should be weighed carefully. A good architect does not guarantee his estimates—and some variance from estimates can be considered normal—but he should be careful not to lead the building committee to expect more than the budget will permit.

A committee has to be cautious in considering an architect who has a special interest in the project, such as being a member of the church or being closely identified with a member of the committee. What is needed is an architect who can view the needs of the church objectively, who can say "no" to a committee without prejudicing his personal relationship with his church, who will view the design not as "my church" but rather as a building designed without personal motivation other than what is normal in a professional relationship.

A committee should not request free competitive sketches to aid in evaluating the architects under consideration. Such sketches, prepared in a relatively short time, would have little value as a measure of ability, and good architects will not prepare free drawings or enter into competition, even if paid, unless the drawings are made in accordance with lengthy and rather costly proceedings recommended by the American Institute of Architects. Furthermore, an architect cannot draw adequate or helpful sketches without full and detailed knowledge of the program of the church.

THE CONSULTING ARCHITECT

A church may wish to employ an unusually talented architect, but distance or other factors may preclude his acceptance of full responsibility for design, preparation of working drawings, and supervision of construction. In such cases, the church and architect may enter into an agreement for architectural services on a consulting basis. The consulting architect will bear full responsibility for a portion of the work, and another architect will be employed to work closely with the consultant and carry out those functions the consultant cannot perform. For instance, a consulting architect might be engaged to develop the over-all design concept, with the local architect being given the responsibility for preparing working drawings and specifications and supervising the construction. In other arrangements, the consulting architect may share in the development of the working drawings and specifications, with the local architect exercising major responsibility for letting of the bids and supervising the construction. Most architects are willing to negotiate fee contracts on this basis, and the combined fee may not be substantially more than the normal percentage charged by one architect who is responsible for the whole job.

THE CONTRACT WITH THE ARCHITECT AND HIS FEES

An architect should not be engaged primarily because his fee is the lowest. The American Institute of Architects suggests fair minimum fees; these vary from place to place. No one would engage a doctor primarily on the basis of his fee, and the same applies here. In the end, any fee paid an incompetent architect is costly, whereas a good architect is invaluable in the service he renders to the church. Normally, the fee is a percentage of the construction cost.

The architect in his initial interview should describe the type of contract his office prefers to use. Some architects have their own forms. Others use forms suggested by professional organizations, such as the form recommended by the American Institute of Architects, known as Document B-131.

The church and the architect may wish to consider amendments to any form of agreement that is proposed. The Committee on Religious Architecture of the AIA has recommended two changes in the AIA form to include, as part of the architect's services, advising the church on furnishings for the church building and the preparation of a comprehensive site utilization and ultimate facilities plan.*

* As reported in the March, 1965, issue of *The American Institute of Architects Journal,* these amendments are as follows:
"The following additional provisions under Article (3) or (4) are agreed to by the owner and the architect.
"(3.2.3.) or (4.11) The architect shall advise the owner on furnishing the structure including but not limited to artwork, stained glass, sculpture, furnishings, pulpits and similar ritual equipment, seating, carpeting and hangings, musical instruments, fixed kitchen equipment, and classroom and office fittings. The architect shall review and advise the owner on acceptability of objects or furnishings, such as memorial gifts, proposed for the project whether or not specifically designed or obtained through the architect's services.
"(3.2.4.) or (4.12) The architect shall prepare comprehensive site utilization and ultimate facilities plan, hereinafter referred to as the master plan. This shall be based on research carried out by the owner under the direction of the architect, establishing anticipated needs, purposes and broad solutions and the projection

Other matters subject to negotiation are the respective obligations of the architect and the church if the bids exceed the architect's estimate of construction cost by a specified percentage, the respective rights and responsibilities of the parties when further building is done in accordance with the master plan, and the extra fee, if any, to which the architect is entitled for preparing the master plan.

The contract should clearly spell out at what time payments are expected on the fee. The natural divisions in the services of the architect are the signing of the contract, the acceptance by the church of preliminary drawings, the completion of working drawings and specifications, the awarding of the contract, and the steps in the completion of the building. Fees are usually paid in accordance with these categories of the architect's services, although the way this is broken down varies.

Regardless of the terms, a contract is no better than the people behind it. Mutual trust and confidence are prerequisites to a satisfactory building program. The relationship of the architect to the church is a personal and professional one. Both the architect and the church come with special talents and responsibilities. It is incumbent on each to see that the contract is executed in accordance with the spirit of this relationship rather than the technical wording of agreements and forms.

IV: FINANCING THE BUILDING PROGRAM

While other study committees are preparing their reports on the needs of the congregation, the Finance Committee should carefully review the financial strength of the church and develop plans to secure the funds needed for the building enterprise. Its principal findings, obviously, need to be included in the written document that is finally approved as the building program.

In most situations, one or more solicitations for capital funds pledges are required. The pledges seldom total enough to underwrite the entire building debt, but they can provide a reliable measure of the church's financial strength. Since the pledges are solicited for a designated purpose, the money received in payment of the pledges should be accounted for separately from funds received for current operations, and should be used only for building and the retirement of building debts.

---

of these on the required master plan. These services shall further include the preparation of a statement of probable project construction cost and either a model or a rendered perspective or both as authorized by the owner for promotional use, and the architect shall further prepare lantern slides or other similar interpretative aids and make presentation in behalf of the owner of the master plan."

(Optional insertion) "The architect shall receive a fee for the master plan except that the prorated portion of the compensation due the architect for services under this article (3.2.4.) or (4.12) shall be credited to the fee for basic services subsequently performed as each stage of the construction is undertaken."

After the building is erected, many churches find they can include their building debt payments in their regular budget. However, if the monthly payments required to meet mortgage obligations are large, it has often been necessary to remain on a "two-pledge" system, with periodic recanvasses for building pledges until the debt is substantially retired. In either event, the members are exepcted to continue giving toward debt retirement after the expiration of the initial building pledges. Unless the first pledge drive can provide substantial funds to retire *all* of the building debt, it is important for the church leaders to emphasize from the outset that followup solicitations will be made, either for increased giving to support a unified budget or for separate building pledges until the entire debt is paid.

Some churches approach a capital funds project with a sense of resignation that the project is undertaken solely out of duty, but this attitude is not an inevitable part of a capital funds program. Projects of this type can provide a framework for an adventuresome experience in Christian stewardship. Just as preparation of a written building program can launch a church into a creative re-examination of mission and purpose, a capital funds project can be the means by which it comes to realize the full dimensions of stewardship. If the emphasis is on stewardship and not upon the dollars needed for the building, the long-term results can be seen in increased giving to all portions of the budget and in new vitality in every area of the church's life.

"OUTSIDE" DIRECTORS FOR CAPITAL FUNDS PROJECTS

Capital funds projects are complex and require considerable organization and know-how. Most churches have concluded that the task is best performed when the project is led by a professional who specializes in this work and is not connected with the local church. His experience in other situations enables him to analyze the situation and help the church avoid procedures that can lead to unsatisfactory results or costly delays. The outside director encourages the church to focus its energies and talents in the direction of the campaign and thus solve the problems posed by the all-too-typical church that has too many chiefs and too few Indians. The objectivity and professional concern of the director will enable him to say things that need to be said but which the minister is less free to say. The director will come with authority, and his counsel will be validated by his experience. When he leaves he can sometimes serve effectively and creatively as the "scapegoat" toward whom all the tensions frequently associated with a building program can be directed.

Statistics and the testimony of many churches establish quite clearly that churches should not attempt to conduct their own financing projects except in those situations where the needs are modest and the church has previously reached a high level of stewardship. In those few churches that can be expected to conduct self-directed campaigns successfully, the committee responsible for the project will still want to secure from denominational or other sources several copies of a good manual that describes in detail recommended procedures for capital funds projects.* Unless this manual is followed in every particular without compromise, the project can easily fall apart as the church seeks to find an easy way to solve a difficult problem.

An outside director cannot be selected responsibly until careful evaluation of the available sources has been made. Many denominations now offer the services of experienced and trained people who will spend a period of time in the parish working with the congregation in preparation for the project. The amount of time spent in the field varies among denominations, and sometimes is dependent on the size of the church and the goal to be attained. A fee is usually charged that is based either on the goal of the project or the number of weeks the director is working in the parish, or both. The success of denominationally directed projects is normally dependent on the co-operation of laymen in the church who are assigned responsibility for much of the preparatory work and all of the solicitations. This, however, is really an advantage, as broad participation in preparing for a project usually leads to broad-based support for the program.

There are also a number of commercial organizations that will direct such campaigns, and many churches have had extremely good results using these firms. The fee is frequently higher than that charged by denominational leaders, but the director will usually spend a greater amount of time in the parish. Commercial firms have larger staffs than most denominational offices and thus can often provide more services. However, even with the employment of a commercial firm, the director of which can give substantially more administrative supervision than can many of their denominational equivalents, a great deal of follow-up effort is expected from the congregation.

Some commercial organizations promote their services by pointing out that their representative will make all solicitation calls and that little is expected of church members in the way of preparation or work. While this relieves the congregation of considerable responsibility and work, this method has serious disadvantages. When congregational participation is minimized, there is little opportunity for developing a sense of purpose and unity among the members. Everything is centered on a house call by a professional solicitor, and this can lead to high-pressure methods as the solicitor attempts to achieve goals set by his company. Most capital funds directors report that training sessions for canvassers are keys to obtaining the interest of the lay leaders and helping them understand the creative possibilities of Christian stewardship. The elimination of canvass-training sessions forfeits this teaching medium without providing an adequate substitute.

* One manual that has proved helpful to churches in a number of denominations is *Adventures in Church Financing* (revised edition) by Curtis R. Schumacher (published by United Church Board for Homeland Ministries, New York, 1968). Available through most denominational book stores.

In setting the fee for leading a project, it is unwise for either the director or the church to suggest that the fee be based upon a percent of the dollar amount pledged. Such a provision inserts a contingency element in the contract and places the project director under great pressure to raise the money, regardless of its effect on the individual church member and the church. The director should be ensured a role in which he can objectively and fairly discuss stewardship principles without unreasonable emphasis on the success or failure of the church in reaching its goal.

SETTING THE GOAL FOR A PROJECT

The amount of the goal should not be set without first seeking the counsel of the project director. He is best equipped to help the church set a reasonable goal based on the size of its membership, the community in which it is located, its previous record of giving, and its need for new buildings. Very often the goal finally determined for a three-year pledge period is a sum approximately equivalent to three times the annual giving of the church for other local and benevolent purposes.

There is some difference of opinion as to whether a three-year or two-year pledge period is preferable. If the community is well established and the church is experiencing little growth or turnover in membership, most project directors agree that three years is the appropriate pledge period. However, if there has been growth and a number of new families can be expected to become members in the ensuing two years, or if the church is undergoing substantial turnover in membership (thus making a three-year pledge relatively meaningless), some argue that a two-year pledge is better strategy. The shorter pledge period enables the church to conduct an intensive recanvass for pledges at an earlier date and thus involve the newer members of the church in a concentrated stewardship program. In any event, regardless of whether it extends over a two- or three-year period, the pledge should be for a *weekly* gift.

Some capital funds directors advocate an "open end" goal. They state that a definite goal not only restricts large giving but is contrary to the ideal of Christian stewardship, in that people ought to be asked to give solely because of their commitment to the church and its program, not to reach a monetary goal. Others claim that goals really do not restrict giving, but may even challenge people to give more generously, that there is a psychological factor involved when a congregation achieves or exceeds a given amount, and that an announced goal relieves the project director of constant explanations ("But what is your real target?") to those who want to know all the details of the program they are being asked to support.

PRELIMINARY BUILDING PLANS

Fund-raisers differ in their recommendations on whether preliminary drawings should be prepared in advance of the stewardship project. Those opposed to preparing building plans in advance point out that plans are usually modified after a project is begun and that until the amount of money available is known, the architect and the building committee are working with inadequate information in developing any plans. Some parishioners will find fault with the plans and use this as an excuse for not pledging, or the fund drive may be unreasonably delayed while plans are prepared. Poor design may be the result when pressure is put on the architect to have plans prepared in advance of the capital funds project.

Those who favor having preliminary sketches before the project gets under way believe it is easier to elevate sights when an individual is enthusiastic, has had the opportunity to resolve his objections to the plans, and is no longer in doubt as to what the church is proposing to do. Congregational approval given to the building plans in advance of the project is admittedly tentative; only after the results of the fund-raising drive are known can final decisions be made. The cost of changing preliminary drawings is usually minimal and is far outweighed by the favorable climate generated when churches have successfully passed the critical point of reaching substantial agreement on the design of the new building.

Since there is no clear resolution of this question, a church is best advised to follow the recommendations of the project director and have plans prepared prior to the project if he believes this to be the preferred procedure.

SHORT-CUT METHODS: A TRAP TO BE AVOIDED

Churches can show remarkable ingenuity in attempting to avoid the financial cost of Christian stewardship! Many programs have been devised to help a church painlessly meet its financial responsibilities, including life insurance schemes, co-signing by "selected" trustees on bank notes, selling bonds to members of the congregation, etc. But any proposal that promises to build a church without asking the members to contribute should be examined with great skepticism.

Selling bonds is a popular device; in some situations such programs have worked out well, especially when the bonds are sold to third parties. However, a bond program does not eliminate the need for a capital funds program. Unless the church has building-fund pledges to underwrite the retirement of a substantial portion of the bonds, it is unlikely that it will accumulate sufficient funds to retire the bonds on schedule.

A much more serious problem is presented when bonds are sold to members of the congregation. Unless such a sale is accompanied by a solicitation of building-fund pledges, the members who purchase bonds are apt to forget that they really have made no contribution to the church by their purchase. They have become lenders who have entered into a commercial arrangement with a debtor, the church. Purchase of the bonds must not be confused in any way with stewardship obligations. Bondholders who are members must still make a substantial over-and-above gift to the church; otherwise the church will not have the funds to retire the bonds when due.

Life insurance programs have been developed that on the surface seem to offer painless ways by which a church may finance new buildings, but they are often complex and difficult to understand. Frequently there are hidden costs which are glossed over in presenting the proposal, and invariably these proposals attempt to do what simply cannot be done— build a church that costs no one any money!

As a general rule, all short cuts that do not challenge the members to commit a portion of their resources to the building program should be avoided. There is no substitute for a generous pledge made after a thoughtful review of one's Christian steward obligation.

BORROWING FROM BANKS AND OTHERS

After the completion of the capital funds project, the finance committee must analyze the financial ability of the church and estimate what amount must be borrowed to erect the building. Few building programs are completed today without some borrowing from denominational or banking sources. The committee should review its current commitments, analyze its needs for new buildings, and chart its future course. (See Work Sheet for Building Debt Analysis, Appendix I, page 145.) Plans need to be made to visit one or more banks and seek their financial support.

The most obvious bank or banks to be approached are those with which the church has established its credit as a depositor or previous borrower. Timing is important. To ask for a commitment prematurely is a serious mistake and can result in a negative response that could have been avoided if the request had been thoroughly prepared and presented at a more appropriate time. However, churches can also wait too long before cultivating the respect and co-operation of banks. As the plans for the building program begin to take shape, a committee appointed for this purpose should establish contact with banks for the sole purpose of keeping them informed on developments within the church. No commitment is asked for at this point and none can possibly be given until plans are developed beyond a preliminary stage. Most banks welcome the opportunity to know what is being projected, however.

The persons delegated to present an application to a bank should make an appointment with the top local official. While he may refer the committee to a junior officer, it is never a mistake for a church to begin at the top. Those representing the church at the interview ought to be well known and financially responsible. Banks will naturally listen with extra care to requests made by men of financial substance who are also identified with the church's building program. A committee of three, two of whom are laymen familiar with the local church's finances and who are also customers or potential customers of the bank, together with the pastor, makes an ideal group for this task.

The approach to the bank must be strictly on a business basis, with no implication of a community responsibility on the part of the bank to make an exception to established rules in order to benefit a church. The application should argue that the church loan is a sound investment and that the bank is to make the loan on this basis and none other.

The preparation of the loan application is extremely important. No request will get a serious hearing unless it is accompanied by careful, painstaking documentation. Facts and figures need to be accurate and up-to-date, and supporting information presented in a logical order and an attractive manner.

Some of the documents that should be included are:

1. Reasonably current title report on the property of the church. If the title has not been reviewed in recent years, an up-to-date report should be obtained, indicating that the church is able to give a merchantable title as security. If there are existing mortgages on the property, written assurances ought to be attached, stating that they will be subordinated, or explaining how these mortgages will be discharged prior to completion of the bank loan.

2. Set of building plans.

3. Balance sheet of the church's finances showing current assets and liabilities and reflecting the net worth of the church.

4. Copy of the current operation and benevolence budget.

5. Statement of the previous year's income and disbursements.

6. Report of the building-fund account from beginning to date, showing the total amount of capital funds pledges made, the cash received and disbursements made, current balance, and where funds are deposited or invested.

7. List of persons who have pledged to the building fund, although this need not include an itemization of the amounts pledged by each person unless this is specifically requested.

8. Copy of the membership roll of the church and a current list of church officers.

9. If available, copies of correspondence from denominational boards or agencies expressing approval of the building project and confidence in the financial future of the church.

10. "Flow of Money" chart (either in graphic form or in columnar tables, see page 161). This chart should show all monies received and disbursed by the church for all purposes (operation, benevolent, and capital) over the previous five- to ten-year period.

11. Month-by-month projection of building-fund expenditures and in-

come, including a schedule for repayment of the bank loan (see pages 162–163). This projection chart should be developed so that it can answer most of the bank's questions at a glance. It is the most useful single tool a church can present, not only for the information of the banks, but to assure church members that their affairs are being handled in a financially competent manner.

12. Covering letter transmitting the above documents.

The most common form of financing is a loan secured by a mortgage or deed of trust on the real property of the church. In addition to banks, mortgage loans are made by some savings and loan companies, some insurance companies, a few individuals, and some denominational boards and agencies. Repayment is expected over a period of time, with payments at regular intervals, usually monthly. Interest is charged in an amount that varies considerably from time to time, and between different sections of the country.

The rules under which denominational loans may be authorized vary greatly. Each church should make inquiry of its own denomination to ascertain whether funds are available and what the requirements are for this type of loan. Banks will sometimes offer to make short-term construction loans in anticipation of a denomination loan to be consummated at the completion of the building.

Occasionally, banks are willing to lend money to churches based on an assignment of building-fund pledges. This type of loan may also be secured by a mortgage against the real property, but more often it is a supplementary loan made in addition to a previously negotiated mortgage loan. "Pledge loans" usually become necessary because the church has incurred unexpected expenses in completing its building, has underestimated the costs involved in building, or wishes to authorize certain "extras" as additions to the building contract. Pledge loans can place a church in financial jeopardy, since they constitute a first claim against the pledge income of the church and are often based on a very rapid rate of amortization. Thus, the church may be left without funds to pay the interest and principal obligations owing on the mortgage indebtedness. If for some reason the church should experience an extraordinary shrinkage in the building pledges, the financial situation can become really acute, inasmuch as the church is without funds to meet either the pledge loan or its other mortgage debt. No church ought to enter into a pledge-loan arrangement without first analyzing all of the risks attendant on this action.

Some banks may refuse to authorize mortgage loans unless the mortgage security is supplemented by a specified number of persons co-signing or guaranteeing payment of the mortgage note. It is seldom advisable for a church to accept financing under these conditions. The corporation seeking the loan is the local church, not a select group of individual members. The financial condition and prospects of the church itself should be sufficient guarantees of performance. Notes co-signed by members can prove embarrassing if the member withdraws from the church or moves from the community. Notes also constitute an item that the co-signing member must list in his private financial reports; this can occasionally make it difficult for him to negotiate needed private credit because of his contingent liability on the church loan.

Sometimes a church can successfully "shop" for the lowest interest rate available. This can be determined by quietly inquiring what interest rate businesses and other churches in the community have been paying. Members of the church with experience in dealing with large sums can prove helpful at this point. Terms of repayment of the loan may be considered more important in some situations than the rate of interest, but care must be exercised. A variation of only a fraction of a point can make a substantial difference in the total cost of the loan over a period of years.

FLOW OF MONEY

THROUGH FIRST CHURCH OF _____

Year	Total Home Expense and Benevolence Receipts	Total Capital Funds Received	Grand Total
1963	$ 9,761	$ 8,805	$ 18,566
1964	14,768	16,928	31,696
1965	19,875	20,534	40,409
1966	20,695	23,884	44,579
1967	28,064	18,377	46,441
1968	30,000	21,002	51,002
Total	$140,748	$109,530	$323,344

Year	Total Membership
1963	256
1964	311
1965	336
1966	482
1967	487
1968	661

Number of Contributing Families	(1968)	284
Number of Families	(1968)	310

30-MONTH BUILDING-FUND PROJECTION FIRST CHURCH OF

| | INCOME | | | DISBURSEMENTS | | | | | | |
Date	Pledges	Bank Loan	Total Income	Architect	Builder	Furnishings	Landscape and Paving	Bank Payoff *	Total Disbursements	Monthly Balance
Mar	$15,800		$ 15,800	$2,800					$2,800	$13,000
Apr	1,600		1,600	2,600					2,600	12,000
May	1,600		1,600		$10,000				10,000	3,600
June	1,600	$13,700	15,300		18,000				18,000	900
July	1,600	16,700	18,300		18,000				18,000	1,200
Aug	1,600	16,700	18,300		18,000				18,000	1,500
Sep	1,600	8,500	10,300		10,000				10,000	1,800
Oct	1,600	10,940	12,540	1,300	9,230	$1,800			12,330	2,010
Nov	1,600	3,460	5,060		2,960		$4,000		6,960	110
Dec	1,600		1,600					$ 1,300	1,300	410
Jan	1,600		1,600					1,300	1,300	710
Feb	1,600		1,600					1,300	1,300	1,010
Mar	1,600		1,600					1,300	1,300	1,310
Apr	1,600		1,600					1,300	1,300	1,610

1968

1969	May	1,600		1,600					1,300	1,910
	June	1,600		1,600					1,300	2,210
	July	1,600		1,600					1,300	2,510
	Aug	1,600		1,600					1,300	2,810
	Sep	1,600		1,600					1,300	3,110
	Oct	1,600		1,600					1,300	3,410
	Nov	1,600		1,600					1,300	3,710
	Dec	1,600		1,600					1,300	4,010
1970	Jan	1,600		1,600					4,300**	1,310
	Feb	1,600		1,600					1,300	1,610
	Mar	1,600		1,600					1,300	1,910
	Apr	1,600		1,600					1,300	2,210
	May	1,600		1,600					1,300	2,510
	June	1,600		1,600					1,300	2,810
	July	1,600		1,600					1,300	3,110
	Aug	1,600		1,600					1,300	3,410
	Totals	$62,200	$64,000	$132,400	$6,700	$83,230	$4,760	$4,000	$30,300	$128,990

* Loan from bank totaling $64,000 repayable at $1,300 per month, including interest.

** Includes prepayment of $3,000.

---❦ ✲ ❧---

Bibliography

Addleshaw, G. W. O., and Frederick Etchelle. *The Architectural Setting of Anglican Worship.* London: 1956.

    Classic review and commentary of broader interest than title would indicate.

Adventures in Church Financing. United Church Board for Homeland Ministries, 287 Park Ave. So., New York, N.Y. 10010.

    This manual describes procedures for capital funds stewardship projects.

Biéler, André, *Architecture in Worship.* Translated by Donald and Odette Elliot. Philadelphia: Westminster Press, 1965.

    Concise sketch of the historical relationship between the theology of worship and the architectural concept of Christian churches.

Bruggink, Donald J., and C. H. Droppers. *Christ and Architecture: Building Presbyterian/Reformed Churches.* Grand Rapids, Mich.: Eerdmans, 1965. 690 pages, 270 photographs and line drawings.

    Excellent source book for worship committees of specified or related persuasion.

Christ-Janer, Albert, and Mary Mix Foley. *Modern Church Architecture: A Guide to the Form and Spirit of Twentieth Century Religious Buildings.* New York: McGraw-Hill, 1962.

    Well-illustrated book of essays and commentary of interest to all program committees.

Church Architecture: The Shape of Reform. Washington, D.C.: The Liturgical Conference, 1965. Conference meeting on church architecture, Cleveland, Ohio, Feb. 23–25, 1965.

    Helpful symposium on the effect of Vatican Council II on religious architecture.

The Church's Educational Ministry: A Curriculum Plan. St. Louis, Mo.: Bethany Press, 1965.

    This book has been developed through the co-operative efforts of many denominations working together through the Co-operative Curriculum Project. It aims to provide a source of sound educational and theological value which will also provide practical help to curriculum-developers in the church.

Cully, Iris V. *Christian Worship and Church Education.* Philadelphia: The Westminster Press, 1967.

    This book relates the central act of the total congregational worship to church education at all age levels.

Davies, J. G. *The Architectural Setting of Baptism.* London: Barrie & Rockliff, 1962.

    The only major book on the subject, and generally a most helpful one.

————. *Origin and Development of Early Christian Church Architecture.* New York: Philosophical Library, 1953.

    Careful historical analysis, for Worship Committee.

————. *The Secular Use of Church Buildings.* New York: Seabury Press, 1968. Chapter 7 is especially important for all committees.

    An important scholarly work.

————. *Worship and Mission.* Great Britain: Northumberland Press, 1966.

    Argues for a renewed relationship between two aspects of the church's life which are often compartmentalized.

Debuyst, Frédéric. *Modern Architecture and Christian Celebration.* Richmond, Va.: John Knox Press, 1968.

    Scholarly, easily read study of Christian worship and architecture. Excellent for Worship Committees.

Dix, Dom Gregory. *The Shape of the Liturgy* (2d ed.). London: Dacre Press: Adam & Charles Black, 1945.

    Scholarly study of ancient liturgies that should be useful in understanding forms of worship.

Dixon, John. *Nature and Grace in Art.* Chapel Hill, N.C.: University of North Carolina Press, 1964.

    Discussion of the relation between art and Christianity.

Eversole, Finley (ed.). *Christian Faith and the Contemporary Arts.* New York: Abingdon Press, 1962.

    Excellent essays helpful to Christian Education, Worship, and Executive Building Committees.

Fallaw, Wesner. *Church Education for Tomorrow.* Philadelphia: The Westminster Press, 1960.

    Provocative statement that attempts to answer a perplexing question.

Fiddes, Victor. *The Architectural Requirements of Protestant Worship.* Toronto: Ryerson Press, 1961.

    While deficient in its analysis of Christian education, this slender but helpful book can serve as a good beginning point.

Frey, Edward S. *This Before Architecture.* Jenkintown, Pa.: Foundation Books, 1963.

    Selected articles demonstrating the important relationship between program and belief, and the building that is erected.

Hageman, Howard G. *Pulpit and Table*. Richmond, Va.: John Knox Press, 1962.
> History of worship in the reformed churches.

Hammond, Peter. *Liturgy and Architecture*. New York: Columbia University Press, 1961.
> While overemphasizing the importance of the communion table in the place of worship, this book is a helpful analysis of the relationship between the action of worship and the architecture of the building. Illustrated.

——— (ed.). *Towards a Church Architecture*. London: The Architectural Press, 1962.
> Excellent collection of essays on the relationship of architecture to belief and purpose.

Havighurst, Robert J. *The Educational Mission of the Church*. Philadelphia: The Westminster Press, 1965.
> An exploration and explanation of the educational functions of churches in a pluralistic society.

Hazelton, Roger. *A Theological Approach to Art*. Nashville, Tenn.: Abingdon Press, 1967.
> A significant presentation and discussion of art as disclosure, embodiment, vocation, and celebration. Nontechnical in language, useful for all laymen, especially those on any arts committee.

Hubbard, Celia T. *Let's See, No. 1*. Glen Rock, N.J.: Paulist Press, 1966.
> While written from the Catholic perspective, there is much here for all committees on the use and misuse of the visual arts in religious education.

Kampf, Avram. *Contemporary Synagogue Art*. New York: Union of American Hebrew Congregations, 1966.
> Illustrated commentary on synagogue art, 1945–1965.

Kidder Smith, G. E. *The New Churches of Europe*. New York: Holt, Rinehart and Winston, 1964.
> 921 photographs and line drawings. Best collection of photographs of European churches. Very useful.

McLuhan, Marshall. *Understanding Media: The Extensions of Man*. New York: McGraw-Hill paperback, 1965.
> Modern classic presenting the author's theories of communication.

Maguire, Robert, and Keith Murray. *Modern Churches*. New York: E. P. Dutton, 1965.
> Valuable paperback for Executive Building and Worship committees.

Newton, Eric, and William Neil. *2000 Years of Christian Art*. New York: Harper & Row, 1966.
> Searching dialogue between an art critic and a biblical scholar for whom the history of Christian art is a meeting point.

Pevsner, Nikolaus. *An Outline of European Architecture* (7th ed.). New York: Penguin Books, 1963.

Excellent general history of architecture. Good background material.

Priest's Guide to Parish Worship. Edited by Liturgical Conference. Baltimore: Garamond/Pridemark Press, 1964.

Explains the implications of the Vatican Council's Constitution on the Liturgy.

Rasmussen, Steen Eiler. *Experiencing Architecture* (rev. ed.). Cambridge, Mass.: M.I.T. Press paperback, 1964.

Discusses the simple attributes on which good architecture has always been founded.

Revolution, Place and Symbol. Edited by Rolfe Lanier Hunt. New York, 1969. International Congress on Religion, Architecture and the Visual Arts.

The Journal of the first International Congress on Religion, Architecture and the Visual Arts, New York and Montreal, 1967. Order from Church Planning and Architecture, National Council of Churches, 475 Riverside Drive, New York, N.Y. 10027.

Rose, Stephen C. *The Grass Roots Church.* New York: Holt, Rinehart and Winston, 1966.

Challenging and provocative analysis deserving serious study.

Schaller, Lyle E. *Planning for Protestantism in Urban America.* New York: Abingdon Press, 1965.

Especially good for Survey and Executive Building committees.

Schwarz, Rudolf. *The Church Incarnate.* Chicago: Henry Regnery Co., 1958.

A classic by one of the great architects of recent years, dealing with the relationship between belief and form.

Scully, Vincent, Jr. *Modern Architecture.* New York: George Braziller, 1961.

Attempts to define the historical dimension of modern architecture.

Shinn, Roger L. *The Educational Mission of Our Church.* Boston and Philadelphia: United Church Press, 1962.

Valuable aid in developing new understandings of Christian education.

Sills, Horace S. (ed.). *Grassroots Ecumenicity.* Philadelphia: United Church Press, 1967.

Six case studies in local church consolidation.

A "must" study for any town and country church that is rethinking its program in terms of building needs.

Slusser, Gerald H. *The Local Church in Transition: Theology, Education and Ministry.* Philadelphia: The Westminster Press, 1964.

States the imperative need for more serious attention and time for church education at all age levels. Discusses specific changes that might be possible and suggests how these changes might become a reality.

Sowers, Robert. *Stained Glass: An Architectural Art.* New York: Universe Books, 1965.

Argues against the view of stained glass as a religious art and presents compelling arguments for a new understanding of an ancient art form.

Taylor, Marvin J. (ed.). *Introduction to Christian Education.* Nashville, Tenn.: Abingdon Press, 1966.

Exceptionally well organized, this book covers all major aspects of Christian education. Each chapter has been prepared by a religious educator who is a specialist in his field.

Van der Leeuw, Gerardus. *Sacred and Profane Beauty: The Holy in Art.* Translated by David E. Green. New York: Holt, Rinehart and Winston, 1963.

Argues that the holy has never been absent from the arts, and the arts have never been unresponsive to the holy.

Vieth, Paul H. *Worship in Christian Education.* Philadelphia and Boston: United Church Press, 1965.

An excellent discussion of worship as the most significant element in Christian education. The meaning of worship and education for worship is related to each and every age group from the youngest children to adults.

Webber, George W. *The Congregation in Mission.* New York and Nashville: Abingdon Press, 1964.

Discusses emerging structures for the church in an urban world.

White, James F. *The Cambridge Movement.* Cambridge, England: Cambridge University Press, 1962.

Careful analysis of the nineteenth-century Gothic revival.

————. *Protestant Worship and Church Architecture.* New York: Oxford University Press, 1964.

Excellent exploration of the theological and historical considerations relevant to building for Protestant worship.

————. *The Worldliness of Worship.* New York: Oxford University Press, 1967.

Outlines a liturgical theology relating the worshiping community to man's life in the world.

Widber, Mildred C., and Scott Turner Ritenour. *Focus: Building for Christian Education.* Boston and Philadelphia: Pilgrim Press, 1969. Published for Cooperative Publishers Association.

A "must" book for building committees concerned with needs for Christian education.

Wyckoff, D. Campbell. *How to Evaluate Your Christian Education Program.* Philadelphia: The Westminster Press, 1962.

The plan for "local church appraisal in Christian education" was prepared and pretested in about 50 churches before publication. Practical, usable, and adaptable.

OTHER SOURCES

Children and TV. Bulletin 21-A (1967). Association for Childhood Education, International, 3615 Wisconsin Ave., N.W., Washington, D.C. 20016.

A series of thoughtful articles dealing with television's impact on the child. "Our Children Learn From TV" and "Educational Television and Children" especially relate to this chapter.

Church Builders Briefs, published by Church Planning and Architecture, National Council of Churches, 475 Riverside Drive, New York, N.Y. 10027.

Practical articles on a wide variety of subjects.

The Church for Others, A Quest for Structure for Missionary Congregations. Geneva and New York: World Council of Churches, 1967.

Important study document for all program committees.

Film Strips. Order from denominational offices and National Council of Churches. (See list of addresses, pp. 170–171.)

Massa, Conrad H. *Architectural Implications of Recent Trends in Reformed Liturgy*. The Princeton Seminary Bulletin, LIV, 3, Feb., 1961.

"Planning Schools for Use of Audio-Visual Materials." Pamphlets: 1. Classrooms; 2. Auditoriums; 3. The A-V Instructional Materials Center; 4. Audio-Visual Centers for Colleges and Universities. Washington, D.C.: National Education Association, 1201 16th St., N.W.

Whyte, James A. "A Place for the Preaching of the Word." Reprint of an article from *Churchbuilding* on the purpose and place of the pulpit. Order from Church Planning and Architecture, National Council of Churches, 475 Riverside Drive, New York, N.Y., 10027.

—◦◦{ ❋ }◦◦—

Partial List of Denominational Addresses

NOTE: While the scope of services varies widely among denominations, all church building committees should contact their denominational agencies for counsel on church building matters.

African Methodist Episcopal
  Board of Church Extension
  1535 14th Street N.W.
  Washington, D.C. 20005
American Baptist
  Church Extension and Edifice
  Funds
  Home Mission Societies
  Valley Forge, Pa. 19481
American Lutheran Church
  Division of American Mission
  422 South Fifth Street
  Minneapolis, Minnesota 96215
A.M.E. Zion
  Department of Home Missions
  Brotherhood, Pensions and Relief
  611 East Fourth Street
  Winston Salem, North Carolina
  27101
Assemblies of God
  International Headquarters
  1445 Boonville Avenue
  Springfield, Missouri 65802

Church of the Brethren
  Ministry and Home Mission
  Commission
  1451 Dundee Avenue
  Elgin, Illinois 60120
Church of God
  (Anderson, Indiana)
  Department of Church Building
  P.O. Box 2069
  Anderson, Indiana 46015
Church of the Nazarene
  Department of Home Missions
  General Board
  6401 The Paseo
  Kansas City, Missouri 64131
Cumberland Presbyterian Church
  Board of Missions & Evangel-
  ism
  Box 14149
  Memphis, Tennessee 38104
Disciples of Christ
  110 South Downey Avenue
  Indianapolis, Indiana 46207

Episcopal Church Executive Council
815 Second Avenue
New York, N.Y. 10017

Interdenominational
Church Building and Architecture
National Council of Churches
475 Riverside Drive
New York, N.Y. 10027
The Canadian Council of Churches
40 St. Clair Avenue East
Toronto 7, Ontario, Canada

The Lutheran Church-Missouri Synod
Church Extension Board
Board for Missions in North and South America
210 North Broadway
St. Louis, Missouri 96202

Methodist
Department of Architecture
Board of Missions
475 Riverside Drive
New York, N.Y. 10027

Moravian Church in America
Board of Christian Education and Evangelism
1135 Main Street
Bethlehem, Pa. 18018

National Baptist Convention, U.S.A., Inc.
Home Missions and Evangelism Board
701–703 S. 19th Street
Philadelphia, Pa. 09046

Presbyterian Church in the U.S.
Division of Home Missions
Department of Church Architecture
341 Ponce de Leon Ave. N.E.
Atlanta, Georgia 30308

Reformed Church in America
Board of North American Missions
475 Riverside Drive
New York, N.Y. 10027

Roman Catholic
The Liturgical Conference
1330 Massachusetts Avenue, N.W.
Washington, D.C. 20005

General Conference of Seventh Day Adventists
6840 Eastern Avenue N.W.
Washington, D.C. 20012

Southern Baptist
Church of Architecture Dept.
Baptist Sunday School Board
127 Ninth Avenue North
Nashville, Tennessee 37203

Union of American Hebrew Congregations
Commission on Synagogue Administration
838 Fifth Avenue
New York, N.Y. 10021

United Church of Canada
The Committee on Church Architecture
85 St. Clair Ave. E.
Toronto 7, Ontario, Canada

United Church of Christ
Church Building Department
287 Park Avenue South
New York, N.Y. 10010

Lutheran Church in America
Commission on Church Architecture
231 Madison Avenue
New York, N.Y. 10016

United Presbyterian Church in the U.S.A.
Dept. of New Church Development and Building Aid
475 Riverside Drive
New York, N.Y. 10027